C-521   CAREER EXAMINATION SERIES

This is your
PASSBOOK for...

Medical Social Worker

Test Preparation Study Guide
Questions & Answers

NATIONAL LEARNING CORPORATION®

COPYRIGHT NOTICE

This book is SOLELY intended for, is sold ONLY to, and its use is RESTRICTED to individual, bona fide applicants or candidates who qualify by virtue of having seriously filed applications for appropriate license, certificate, professional and/or promotional advancement, higher school matriculation, scholarship, or other legitimate requirements of education and/or governmental authorities.

This book is NOT intended for use, class instruction, tutoring, training, duplication, copying, reprinting, excerption, or adaptation, etc., by:

1) Other publishers
2) Proprietors and/or Instructors of "Coaching" and/or Preparatory Courses
3) Personnel and/or Training Divisions of commercial, industrial, and governmental organizations
4) Schools, colleges, or universities and/or their departments and staffs, including teachers and other personnel
5) Testing Agencies or Bureaus
6) Study groups which seek by the purchase of a single volume to copy and/or duplicate and/or adapt this material for use by the group as a whole without having purchased individual volumes for each of the members of the group
7) Et al.

Such persons would be in violation of appropriate Federal and State statutes.

PROVISION OF LICENSING AGREEMENTS – Recognized educational, commercial, industrial, and governmental institutions and organizations, and others legitimately engaged in educational pursuits, including training, testing, and measurement activities, may address request for a licensing agreement to the copyright owners, who will determine whether, and under what conditions, including fees and charges, the materials in this book may be used them. In other words, a licensing facility exists for the legitimate use of the material in this book on other than an individual basis. However, it is asseverated and affirmed here that the material in this book CANNOT be used without the receipt of the express permission of such a licensing agreement from the Publishers. Inquiries re licensing should be addressed to the company, attention rights and permissions department.

All rights reserved, including the right of reproduction in whole or in part, in any form or by any means, electronic or mechanical, including photocopying, recording, or by any information storage and retrieval system, without permission in writing from the Publisher.

Copyright © 2024 by
National Learning Corporation

212 Michael Drive, Syosset, NY 11791
(516) 921-8888 • www.passbooks.com
E-mail: info@passbooks.com

PUBLISHED IN THE UNITED STATES OF AMERICA

PASSBOOK® SERIES

THE *PASSBOOK® SERIES* has been created to prepare applicants and candidates for the ultimate academic battlefield – the examination room.

At some time in our lives, each and every one of us may be required to take an examination – for validation, matriculation, admission, qualification, registration, certification, or licensure.

Based on the assumption that every applicant or candidate has met the basic formal educational standards, has taken the required number of courses, and read the necessary texts, the *PASSBOOK® SERIES* furnishes the one special preparation which may assure passing with confidence, instead of failing with insecurity. Examination questions – together with answers – are furnished as the basic vehicle for study so that the mysteries of the examination and its compounding difficulties may be eliminated or diminished by a sure method.

This book is meant to help you pass your examination provided that you qualify and are serious in your objective.

The entire field is reviewed through the huge store of content information which is succinctly presented through a provocative and challenging approach – the question-and-answer method.

A climate of success is established by furnishing the correct answers at the end of each test.

You soon learn to recognize types of questions, forms of questions, and patterns of questioning. You may even begin to anticipate expected outcomes.

You perceive that many questions are repeated or adapted so that you can gain acute insights, which may enable you to score many sure points.

You learn how to confront new questions, or types of questions, and to attack them confidently and work out the correct answers.

You note objectives and emphases, and recognize pitfalls and dangers, so that you may make positive educational adjustments.

Moreover, you are kept fully informed in relation to new concepts, methods, practices, and directions in the field.

You discover that you are actually taking the examination all the time: you are preparing for the examination by "taking" an examination, not by reading extraneous and/or supererogatory textbooks.

In short, this PASSBOOK®, used directedly, should be an important factor in helping you to pass your test.

MEDICAL SOCIAL WORKER

DUTIES
An employee in this class performs professional medical social work for patients treated at the County Family Health Centers and Infirmary. Work involves applying specialized social work techniques to the rehabilitation and adjustment of physically ill and/or emotionally disturbed persons. The incumbent works closely with other health care professionals, such as physicians and nurses, in planning treatment for patients, and works with other agencies and community organizations to obtain services and develop resources. Supervision is received from an administrative supervisor through the review of case records and reports, and through individual and staff conferences. Does related work as required.

SCOPE OF THE EXAMINATION
The written test is designed to cover knowledge, skills and/or abilities in such areas as:

1. Understanding and Interpreting Written Material;
2. Preparing Written Material;
3. Medical Terminology; and
4. Social Work Practices and Procedures.

HOW TO TAKE A TEST

I. YOU MUST PASS AN EXAMINATION

A. WHAT EVERY CANDIDATE SHOULD KNOW
Examination applicants often ask us for help in preparing for the written test. What can I study in advance? What kinds of questions will be asked? How will the test be given? How will the papers be graded?

As an applicant for a civil service examination, you may be wondering about some of these things. Our purpose here is to suggest effective methods of advance study and to describe civil service examinations.

Your chances for success on this examination can be increased if you know how to prepare. Those "pre-examination jitters" can be reduced if you know what to expect. You can even experience an adventure in good citizenship if you know why civil service exams are given.

B. WHY ARE CIVIL SERVICE EXAMINATIONS GIVEN?
Civil service examinations are important to you in two ways. As a citizen, you want public jobs filled by employees who know how to do their work. As a job seeker, you want a fair chance to compete for that job on an equal footing with other candidates. The best-known means of accomplishing this two-fold goal is the competitive examination.

Exams are widely publicized throughout the nation. They may be administered for jobs in federal, state, city, municipal, town or village governments or agencies.

Any citizen may apply, with some limitations, such as the age or residence of applicants. Your experience and education may be reviewed to see whether you meet the requirements for the particular examination. When these requirements exist, they are reasonable and applied consistently to all applicants. Thus, a competitive examination may cause you some uneasiness now, but it is your privilege and safeguard.

C. HOW ARE CIVIL SERVICE EXAMS DEVELOPED?
Examinations are carefully written by trained technicians who are specialists in the field known as "psychological measurement," in consultation with recognized authorities in the field of work that the test will cover. These experts recommend the subject matter areas or skills to be tested; only those knowledges or skills important to your success on the job are included. The most reliable books and source materials available are used as references. Together, the experts and technicians judge the difficulty level of the questions.

Test technicians know how to phrase questions so that the problem is clearly stated. Their ethics do not permit "trick" or "catch" questions. Questions may have been tried out on sample groups, or subjected to statistical analysis, to determine their usefulness.

Written tests are often used in combination with performance tests, ratings of training and experience, and oral interviews. All of these measures combine to form the best-known means of finding the right person for the right job.

II. HOW TO PASS THE WRITTEN TEST

A. NATURE OF THE EXAMINATION

To prepare intelligently for civil service examinations, you should know how they differ from school examinations you have taken. In school you were assigned certain definite pages to read or subjects to cover. The examination questions were quite detailed and usually emphasized memory. Civil service exams, on the other hand, try to discover your present ability to perform the duties of a position, plus your potentiality to learn these duties. In other words, a civil service exam attempts to predict how successful you will be. Questions cover such a broad area that they cannot be as minute and detailed as school exam questions.

In the public service similar kinds of work, or positions, are grouped together in one "class." This process is known as *position-classification*. All the positions in a class are paid according to the salary range for that class. One class title covers all of these positions, and they are all tested by the same examination.

B. FOUR BASIC STEPS

1) Study the announcement

How, then, can you know what subjects to study? Our best answer is: "Learn as much as possible about the class of positions for which you've applied." The exam will test the knowledge, skills and abilities needed to do the work.

Your most valuable source of information about the position you want is the official exam announcement. This announcement lists the training and experience qualifications. Check these standards and apply only if you come reasonably close to meeting them.

The brief description of the position in the examination announcement offers some clues to the subjects which will be tested. Think about the job itself. Review the duties in your mind. Can you perform them, or are there some in which you are rusty? Fill in the blank spots in your preparation.

Many jurisdictions preview the written test in the exam announcement by including a section called "Knowledge and Abilities Required," "Scope of the Examination," or some similar heading. Here you will find out specifically what fields will be tested.

2) Review your own background

Once you learn in general what the position is all about, and what you need to know to do the work, ask yourself which subjects you already know fairly well and which need improvement. You may wonder whether to concentrate on improving your strong areas or on building some background in your fields of weakness. When the announcement has specified "some knowledge" or "considerable knowledge," or has used adjectives like "beginning principles of…" or "advanced … methods," you can get a clue as to the number and difficulty of questions to be asked in any given field. More questions, and hence broader coverage, would be included for those subjects which are more important in the work. Now weigh your strengths and weaknesses against the job requirements and prepare accordingly.

3) Determine the level of the position

Another way to tell how intensively you should prepare is to understand the level of the job for which you are applying. Is it the entering level? In other words, is this the position in which beginners in a field of work are hired? Or is it an intermediate or advanced level? Sometimes this is indicated by such words as "Junior" or "Senior" in the class title. Other jurisdictions use Roman numerals to designate the level – Clerk I, Clerk II, for example. The word "Supervisor" sometimes appears in the title. If the level is not indicated by the title, check the description of duties. Will you be working under very close supervision, or will you have responsibility for independent decisions in this work?

4) Choose appropriate study materials

Now that you know the subjects to be examined and the relative amount of each subject to be covered, you can choose suitable study materials. For beginning level jobs, or even advanced ones, if you have a pronounced weakness in some aspect of your training, read a modern, standard textbook in that field. Be sure it is up to date and has general coverage. Such books are normally available at your library, and the librarian will be glad to help you locate one. For entry-level positions, questions of appropriate difficulty are chosen – neither highly advanced questions, nor those too simple. Such questions require careful thought but not advanced training.

If the position for which you are applying is technical or advanced, you will read more advanced, specialized material. If you are already familiar with the basic principles of your field, elementary textbooks would waste your time. Concentrate on advanced textbooks and technical periodicals. Think through the concepts and review difficult problems in your field.

These are all general sources. You can get more ideas on your own initiative, following these leads. For example, training manuals and publications of the government agency which employs workers in your field can be useful, particularly for technical and professional positions. A letter or visit to the government department involved may result in more specific study suggestions, and certainly will provide you with a more definite idea of the exact nature of the position you are seeking.

III. KINDS OF TESTS

Tests are used for purposes other than measuring knowledge and ability to perform specified duties. For some positions, it is equally important to test ability to make adjustments to new situations or to profit from training. In others, basic mental abilities not dependent on information are essential. Questions which test these things may not appear as pertinent to the duties of the position as those which test for knowledge and information. Yet they are often highly important parts of a fair examination. For very general questions, it is almost impossible to help you direct your study efforts. What we can do is to point out some of the more common of these general abilities needed in public service positions and describe some typical questions.

1) General information

Broad, general information has been found useful for predicting job success in some kinds of work. This is tested in a variety of ways, from vocabulary lists to questions about current events. Basic background in some field of work, such as sociology or economics, may be sampled in a group of questions. Often these are principles which have become familiar to most persons through exposure rather than through formal training. It is difficult to advise you how to study for these questions; being alert to the world around you is our best suggestion.

2) Verbal ability

An example of an ability needed in many positions is verbal or language ability. Verbal ability is, in brief, the ability to use and understand words. Vocabulary and grammar tests are typical measures of this ability. Reading comprehension or paragraph interpretation questions are common in many kinds of civil service tests. You are given a paragraph of written material and asked to find its central meaning.

3) Numerical ability

Number skills can be tested by the familiar arithmetic problem, by checking paired lists of numbers to see which are alike and which are different, or by interpreting charts and graphs. In the latter test, a graph may be printed in the test booklet which you are asked to use as the basis for answering questions.

4) Observation

A popular test for law-enforcement positions is the observation test. A picture is shown to you for several minutes, then taken away. Questions about the picture test your ability to observe both details and larger elements.

5) Following directions

In many positions in the public service, the employee must be able to carry out written instructions dependably and accurately. You may be given a chart with several columns, each column listing a variety of information. The questions require you to carry out directions involving the information given in the chart.

6) Skills and aptitudes

Performance tests effectively measure some manual skills and aptitudes. When the skill is one in which you are trained, such as typing or shorthand, you can practice. These tests are often very much like those given in business school or high school courses. For many of the other skills and aptitudes, however, no short-time preparation can be made. Skills and abilities natural to you or that you have developed throughout your lifetime are being tested.

Many of the general questions just described provide all the data needed to answer the questions and ask you to use your reasoning ability to find the answers. Your best preparation for these tests, as well as for tests of facts and ideas, is to be at your physical and mental best. You, no doubt, have your own methods of getting into an exam-taking mood and keeping "in shape." The next section lists some ideas on this subject.

IV. KINDS OF QUESTIONS

Only rarely is the "essay" question, which you answer in narrative form, used in civil service tests. Civil service tests are usually of the short-answer type. Full instructions for answering these questions will be given to you at the examination. But in case this is your first experience with short-answer questions and separate answer sheets, here is what you need to know:

1) Multiple-choice Questions

Most popular of the short-answer questions is the "multiple choice" or "best answer" question. It can be used, for example, to test for factual knowledge, ability to solve problems or judgment in meeting situations found at work.

A multiple-choice question is normally one of three types—
- It can begin with an incomplete statement followed by several possible endings. You are to find the one ending which *best* completes the statement, although some of the others may not be entirely wrong.
- It can also be a complete statement in the form of a question which is answered by choosing one of the statements listed.

- It can be in the form of a problem – again you select the best answer.

Here is an example of a multiple-choice question with a discussion which should give you some clues as to the method for choosing the right answer:

When an employee has a complaint about his assignment, the action which will *best* help him overcome his difficulty is to
- A. discuss his difficulty with his coworkers
- B. take the problem to the head of the organization
- C. take the problem to the person who gave him the assignment
- D. say nothing to anyone about his complaint

In answering this question, you should study each of the choices to find which is best. Consider choice "A" – Certainly an employee may discuss his complaint with fellow employees, but no change or improvement can result, and the complaint remains unresolved. Choice "B" is a poor choice since the head of the organization probably does not know what assignment you have been given, and taking your problem to him is known as "going over the head" of the supervisor. The supervisor, or person who made the assignment, is the person who can clarify it or correct any injustice. Choice "C" is, therefore, correct. To say nothing, as in choice "D," is unwise. Supervisors have and interest in knowing the problems employees are facing, and the employee is seeking a solution to his problem.

2) True/False Questions

The "true/false" or "right/wrong" form of question is sometimes used. Here a complete statement is given. Your job is to decide whether the statement is right or wrong.

SAMPLE: A roaming cell-phone call to a nearby city costs less than a non-roaming call to a distant city.

This statement is wrong, or false, since roaming calls are more expensive.

This is not a complete list of all possible question forms, although most of the others are variations of these common types. You will always get complete directions for answering questions. Be sure you understand *how* to mark your answers – ask questions until you do.

V. RECORDING YOUR ANSWERS

Computer terminals are used more and more today for many different kinds of exams.
For an examination with very few applicants, you may be told to record your answers in the test booklet itself. Separate answer sheets are much more common. If this separate answer sheet is to be scored by machine – and this is often the case – it is highly important that you mark your answers correctly in order to get credit.

An electronic scoring machine is often used in civil service offices because of the speed with which papers can be scored. Machine-scored answer sheets must be marked with a pencil, which will be given to you. This pencil has a high graphite content which responds to the electronic scoring machine. As a matter of fact, stray dots may register as answers, so do not let your pencil rest on the answer sheet while you are pondering the correct answer. Also, if your pencil lead breaks or is otherwise defective, ask for another.

Since the answer sheet will be dropped in a slot in the scoring machine, be careful not to bend the corners or get the paper crumpled.

The answer sheet normally has five vertical columns of numbers, with 30 numbers to a column. These numbers correspond to the question numbers in your test booklet. After each number, going across the page are four or five pairs of dotted lines. These short dotted lines have small letters or numbers above them. The first two pairs may also have a "T" or "F" above the letters. This indicates that the first two pairs only are to be used if the questions are of the true-false type. If the questions are multiple choice, disregard the "T" and "F" and pay attention only to the small letters or numbers.

Answer your questions in the manner of the sample that follows:

32. The largest city in the United States is
    A. Washington, D.C.
    B. New York City
    C. Chicago
    D. Detroit
    E. San Francisco

1) Choose the answer you think is best. (New York City is the largest, so "B" is correct.)
2) Find the row of dotted lines numbered the same as the question you are answering. (Find row number 32)
3) Find the pair of dotted lines corresponding to the answer. (Find the pair of lines under the mark "B.")
4) Make a solid black mark between the dotted lines.

VI. BEFORE THE TEST

Common sense will help you find procedures to follow to get ready for an examination. Too many of us, however, overlook these sensible measures. Indeed, nervousness and fatigue have been found to be the most serious reasons why applicants fail to do their best on civil service tests. Here is a list of reminders:

- Begin your preparation early – Don't wait until the last minute to go scurrying around for books and materials or to find out what the position is all about.
- Prepare continuously – An hour a night for a week is better than an all-night cram session. This has been definitely established. What is more, a night a week for a month will return better dividends than crowding your study into a shorter period of time.
- Locate the place of the exam – You have been sent a notice telling you when and where to report for the examination. If the location is in a different town or otherwise unfamiliar to you, it would be well to inquire the best route and learn something about the building.
- Relax the night before the test – Allow your mind to rest. Do not study at all that night. Plan some mild recreation or diversion; then go to bed early and get a good night's sleep.
- Get up early enough to make a leisurely trip to the place for the test – This way unforeseen events, traffic snarls, unfamiliar buildings, etc. will not upset you.
- Dress comfortably – A written test is not a fashion show. You will be known by number and not by name, so wear something comfortable.

- Leave excess paraphernalia at home – Shopping bags and odd bundles will get in your way. You need bring only the items mentioned in the official notice you received; usually everything you need is provided. Do not bring reference books to the exam. They will only confuse those last minutes and be taken away from you when in the test room.
- Arrive somewhat ahead of time – If because of transportation schedules you must get there very early, bring a newspaper or magazine to take your mind off yourself while waiting.
- Locate the examination room – When you have found the proper room, you will be directed to the seat or part of the room where you will sit. Sometimes you are given a sheet of instructions to read while you are waiting. Do not fill out any forms until you are told to do so; just read them and be prepared.
- Relax and prepare to listen to the instructions
- If you have any physical problem that may keep you from doing your best, be sure to tell the test administrator. If you are sick or in poor health, you really cannot do your best on the exam. You can come back and take the test some other time.

VII. AT THE TEST

The day of the test is here and you have the test booklet in your hand. The temptation to get going is very strong. Caution! There is more to success than knowing the right answers. You must know how to identify your papers and understand variations in the type of short-answer question used in this particular examination. Follow these suggestions for maximum results from your efforts:

1) Cooperate with the monitor

The test administrator has a duty to create a situation in which you can be as much at ease as possible. He will give instructions, tell you when to begin, check to see that you are marking your answer sheet correctly, and so on. He is not there to guard you, although he will see that your competitors do not take unfair advantage. He wants to help you do your best.

2) Listen to all instructions

Don't jump the gun! Wait until you understand all directions. In most civil service tests you get more time than you need to answer the questions. So don't be in a hurry. Read each word of instructions until you clearly understand the meaning. Study the examples, listen to all announcements and follow directions. Ask questions if you do not understand what to do.

3) Identify your papers

Civil service exams are usually identified by number only. You will be assigned a number; you must not put your name on your test papers. Be sure to copy your number correctly. Since more than one exam may be given, copy your exact examination title.

4) Plan your time

Unless you are told that a test is a "speed" or "rate of work" test, speed itself is usually not important. Time enough to answer all the questions will be provided, but this does not mean that you have all day. An overall time limit has been set. Divide the total time (in minutes) by the number of questions to determine the approximate time you have for each question.

5) Do not linger over difficult questions

If you come across a difficult question, mark it with a paper clip (useful to have along) and come back to it when you have been through the booklet. One caution if you do this – be sure to skip a number on your answer sheet as well. Check often to be sure that you have not lost your place and that you are marking in the row numbered the same as the question you are answering.

6) Read the questions

Be sure you know what the question asks! Many capable people are unsuccessful because they failed to *read* the questions correctly.

7) Answer all questions

Unless you have been instructed that a penalty will be deducted for incorrect answers, it is better to guess than to omit a question.

8) Speed tests

It is often better NOT to guess on speed tests. It has been found that on timed tests people are tempted to spend the last few seconds before time is called in marking answers at random – without even reading them – in the hope of picking up a few extra points. To discourage this practice, the instructions may warn you that your score will be "corrected" for guessing. That is, a penalty will be applied. The incorrect answers will be deducted from the correct ones, or some other penalty formula will be used.

9) Review your answers

If you finish before time is called, go back to the questions you guessed or omitted to give them further thought. Review other answers if you have time.

10) Return your test materials

If you are ready to leave before others have finished or time is called, take ALL your materials to the monitor and leave quietly. Never take any test material with you. The monitor can discover whose papers are not complete, and taking a test booklet may be grounds for disqualification.

VIII. EXAMINATION TECHNIQUES

1) Read the general instructions carefully. These are usually printed on the first page of the exam booklet. As a rule, these instructions refer to the timing of the examination; the fact that you should not start work until the signal and must stop work at a signal, etc. If there are any *special* instructions, such as a choice of questions to be answered, make sure that you note this instruction carefully.

2) When you are ready to start work on the examination, that is as soon as the signal has been given, read the instructions to each question booklet, underline any key words or phrases, such as *least, best, outline, describe* and the like. In this way you will tend to answer as requested rather than discover on reviewing your paper that you *listed without describing*, that you selected the *worst* choice rather than the *best* choice, etc.

3) If the examination is of the objective or multiple-choice type – that is, each question will also give a series of possible answers: A, B, C or D, and you are called upon to select the best answer and write the letter next to that answer on your answer paper – it is advisable to start answering each question in turn. There may be anywhere from 50 to 100 such questions in the three or four hours allotted and you can see how much time would be taken if you read through all the questions before beginning to answer any. Furthermore, if you come across a question or group of questions which you know would be difficult to answer, it would undoubtedly affect your handling of all the other questions.

4) If the examination is of the essay type and contains but a few questions, it is a moot point as to whether you should read all the questions before starting to answer any one. Of course, if you are given a choice – say five out of seven and the like – then it is essential to read all the questions so you can eliminate the two that are most difficult. If, however, you are asked to answer all the questions, there may be danger in trying to answer the easiest one first because you may find that you will spend too much time on it. The best technique is to answer the first question, then proceed to the second, etc.

5) Time your answers. Before the exam begins, write down the time it started, then add the time allowed for the examination and write down the time it must be completed, then divide the time available somewhat as follows:
   - If 3-1/2 hours are allowed, that would be 210 minutes. If you have 80 objective-type questions, that would be an average of 2-1/2 minutes per question. Allow yourself no more than 2 minutes per question, or a total of 160 minutes, which will permit about 50 minutes to review.
   - If for the time allotment of 210 minutes there are 7 essay questions to answer, that would average about 30 minutes a question. Give yourself only 25 minutes per question so that you have about 35 minutes to review.

6) The most important instruction is to *read each question* and make sure you know what is wanted. The second most important instruction is to *time yourself properly* so that you answer every question. The third most important instruction is to *answer every question*. Guess if you have to but include something for each question. Remember that you will receive no credit for a blank and will probably receive some credit if you write something in answer to an essay question. If you guess a letter – say "B" for a multiple-choice question – you may have guessed right. If you leave a blank as an answer to a multiple-choice question, the examiners may respect your feelings but it will not add a point to your score. Some exams may penalize you for wrong answers, so in such cases *only*, you may not want to guess unless you have some basis for your answer.

7) Suggestions
   a. Objective-type questions
      1. Examine the question booklet for proper sequence of pages and questions
      2. Read all instructions carefully
      3. Skip any question which seems too difficult; return to it after all other questions have been answered
      4. Apportion your time properly; do not spend too much time on any single question or group of questions

5. Note and underline key words – *all, most, fewest, least, best, worst, same, opposite,* etc.
6. Pay particular attention to negatives
7. Note unusual option, e.g., unduly long, short, complex, different or similar in content to the body of the question
8. Observe the use of "hedging" words – *probably, may, most likely,* etc.
9. Make sure that your answer is put next to the same number as the question
10. Do not second-guess unless you have good reason to believe the second answer is definitely more correct
11. Cross out original answer if you decide another answer is more accurate; do not erase until you are ready to hand your paper in
12. Answer all questions; guess unless instructed otherwise
13. Leave time for review

   b. Essay questions
1. Read each question carefully
2. Determine exactly what is wanted. Underline key words or phrases.
3. Decide on outline or paragraph answer
4. Include many different points and elements unless asked to develop any one or two points or elements
5. Show impartiality by giving pros and cons unless directed to select one side only
6. Make and write down any assumptions you find necessary to answer the questions
7. Watch your English, grammar, punctuation and choice of words
8. Time your answers; don't crowd material

8) Answering the essay question

Most essay questions can be answered by framing the specific response around several key words or ideas. Here are a few such key words or ideas:

M's: manpower, materials, methods, money, management
P's: purpose, program, policy, plan, procedure, practice, problems, pitfalls, personnel, public relations

   a. Six basic steps in handling problems:
1. Preliminary plan and background development
2. Collect information, data and facts
3. Analyze and interpret information, data and facts
4. Analyze and develop solutions as well as make recommendations
5. Prepare report and sell recommendations
6. Install recommendations and follow up effectiveness

   b. Pitfalls to avoid
1. *Taking things for granted* – A statement of the situation does not necessarily imply that each of the elements is necessarily true; for example, a complaint may be invalid and biased so that all that can be taken for granted is that a complaint has been registered

2. *Considering only one side of a situation* – Wherever possible, indicate several alternatives and then point out the reasons you selected the best one
3. *Failing to indicate follow up* – Whenever your answer indicates action on your part, make certain that you will take proper follow-up action to see how successful your recommendations, procedures or actions turn out to be
4. *Taking too long in answering any single question* – Remember to time your answers properly

IX. AFTER THE TEST

Scoring procedures differ in detail among civil service jurisdictions although the general principles are the same. Whether the papers are hand-scored or graded by machine we have described, they are nearly always graded by number. That is, the person who marks the paper knows only the number – never the name – of the applicant. Not until all the papers have been graded will they be matched with names. If other tests, such as training and experience or oral interview ratings have been given, scores will be combined. Different parts of the examination usually have different weights. For example, the written test might count 60 percent of the final grade, and a rating of training and experience 40 percent. In many jurisdictions, veterans will have a certain number of points added to their grades.

After the final grade has been determined, the names are placed in grade order and an eligible list is established. There are various methods for resolving ties between those who get the same final grade – probably the most common is to place first the name of the person whose application was received first. Job offers are made from the eligible list in the order the names appear on it. You will be notified of your grade and your rank as soon as all these computations have been made. This will be done as rapidly as possible.

People who are found to meet the requirements in the announcement are called "eligibles." Their names are put on a list of eligible candidates. An eligible's chances of getting a job depend on how high he stands on this list and how fast agencies are filling jobs from the list.

When a job is to be filled from a list of eligibles, the agency asks for the names of people on the list of eligibles for that job. When the civil service commission receives this request, it sends to the agency the names of the three people highest on this list. Or, if the job to be filled has specialized requirements, the office sends the agency the names of the top three persons who meet these requirements from the general list.

The appointing officer makes a choice from among the three people whose names were sent to him. If the selected person accepts the appointment, the names of the others are put back on the list to be considered for future openings.

That is the rule in hiring from all kinds of eligible lists, whether they are for typist, carpenter, chemist, or something else. For every vacancy, the appointing officer has his choice of any one of the top three eligibles on the list. This explains why the person whose name is on top of the list sometimes does not get an appointment when some of the persons lower on the list do. If the appointing officer chooses the second or third eligible, the No. 1 eligible does not get a job at once, but stays on the list until he is appointed or the list is terminated.

X. HOW TO PASS THE INTERVIEW TEST

The examination for which you applied requires an oral interview test. You have already taken the written test and you are now being called for the interview test – the final part of the formal examination.

You may think that it is not possible to prepare for an interview test and that there are no procedures to follow during an interview. Our purpose is to point out some things you can do in advance that will help you and some good rules to follow and pitfalls to avoid while you are being interviewed.

What is an interview supposed to test?

The written examination is designed to test the technical knowledge and competence of the candidate; the oral is designed to evaluate intangible qualities, not readily measured otherwise, and to establish a list showing the relative fitness of each candidate – as measured against his competitors – for the position sought. Scoring is not on the basis of "right" and "wrong," but on a sliding scale of values ranging from "not passable" to "outstanding." As a matter of fact, it is possible to achieve a relatively low score without a single "incorrect" answer because of evident weakness in the qualities being measured.

Occasionally, an examination may consist entirely of an oral test – either an individual or a group oral. In such cases, information is sought concerning the technical knowledges and abilities of the candidate, since there has been no written examination for this purpose. More commonly, however, an oral test is used to supplement a written examination.

Who conducts interviews?

The composition of oral boards varies among different jurisdictions. In nearly all, a representative of the personnel department serves as chairman. One of the members of the board may be a representative of the department in which the candidate would work. In some cases, "outside experts" are used, and, frequently, a businessman or some other representative of the general public is asked to serve. Labor and management or other special groups may be represented. The aim is to secure the services of experts in the appropriate field.

However the board is composed, it is a good idea (and not at all improper or unethical) to ascertain in advance of the interview who the members are and what groups they represent. When you are introduced to them, you will have some idea of their backgrounds and interests, and at least you will not stutter and stammer over their names.

What should be done before the interview?

While knowledge about the board members is useful and takes some of the surprise element out of the interview, there is other preparation which is more substantive. It *is* possible to prepare for an oral interview – in several ways:

1) Keep a copy of your application and review it carefully before the interview

This may be the only document before the oral board, and the starting point of the interview. Know what education and experience you have listed there, and the sequence and dates of all of it. Sometimes the board will ask you to review the highlights of your experience for them; you should not have to hem and haw doing it.

2) Study the class specification and the examination announcement

Usually, the oral board has one or both of these to guide them. The qualities, characteristics or knowledges required by the position sought are stated in these documents. They offer valuable clues as to the nature of the oral interview. For example, if the job involves supervisory responsibilities, the announcement will usually indicate that knowledge of modern supervisory methods and the qualifications of the candidate as a supervisor will be tested. If so, you can expect such questions, frequently in the form of a hypothetical situation which you are expected to solve. NEVER go into an oral without knowledge of the duties and responsibilities of the job you seek.

3) Think through each qualification required

Try to visualize the kind of questions you would ask if you were a board member. How well could you answer them? Try especially to appraise your own knowledge and background in each area, *measured against the job sought*, and identify any areas in which you are weak. Be critical and realistic – do not flatter yourself.

4) Do some general reading in areas in which you feel you may be weak

For example, if the job involves supervision and your past experience has NOT, some general reading in supervisory methods and practices, particularly in the field of human relations, might be useful. Do NOT study agency procedures or detailed manuals. The oral board will be testing your understanding and capacity, not your memory.

5) Get a good night's sleep and watch your general health and mental attitude

You will want a clear head at the interview. Take care of a cold or any other minor ailment, and of course, no hangovers.

What should be done on the day of the interview?

Now comes the day of the interview itself. Give yourself plenty of time to get there. Plan to arrive somewhat ahead of the scheduled time, particularly if your appointment is in the fore part of the day. If a previous candidate fails to appear, the board might be ready for you a bit early. By early afternoon an oral board is almost invariably behind schedule if there are many candidates, and you may have to wait. Take along a book or magazine to read, or your application to review, but leave any extraneous material in the waiting room when you go in for your interview. In any event, relax and compose yourself.

The matter of dress is important. The board is forming impressions about you – from your experience, your manners, your attitude, and your appearance. Give your personal appearance careful attention. Dress your best, but not your flashiest. Choose conservative, appropriate clothing, and be sure it is immaculate. This is a business interview, and your appearance should indicate that you regard it as such. Besides, being well groomed and properly dressed will help boost your confidence.

Sooner or later, someone will call your name and escort you into the interview room. *This is it.* From here on you are on your own. It is too late for any more preparation. But remember, you asked for this opportunity to prove your fitness, and you are here because your request was granted.

What happens when you go in?

The usual sequence of events will be as follows: The clerk (who is often the board stenographer) will introduce you to the chairman of the oral board, who will introduce you to the other members of the board. Acknowledge the introductions before you sit down. Do not be surprised if you find a microphone facing you or a stenotypist sitting by. Oral interviews are usually recorded in the event of an appeal or other review.

Usually the chairman of the board will open the interview by reviewing the highlights of your education and work experience from your application – primarily for the benefit of the other members of the board, as well as to get the material into the record. Do not interrupt or comment unless there is an error or significant misinterpretation; if that is the case, do not hesitate. But do not quibble about insignificant matters. Also, he will usually ask you some question about your education, experience or your present job – partly to get you to start talking and to establish the interviewing "rapport." He may start the actual questioning, or turn it over to one of the other members. Frequently, each member undertakes the questioning on a particular area, one in which he is perhaps most competent, so you can expect each member to participate in the examination. Because time is limited, you may also expect some rather abrupt switches in the direction the questioning takes, so do not be upset by it. Normally, a board member will not pursue a single line of questioning unless he discovers a particular strength or weakness.

After each member has participated, the chairman will usually ask whether any member has any further questions, then will ask you if you have anything you wish to add. Unless you are expecting this question, it may floor you. Worse, it may start you off on an extended, extemporaneous speech. The board is not usually seeking more information. The question is principally to offer you a last opportunity to present further qualifications or to indicate that you have nothing to add. So, if you feel that a significant qualification or characteristic has been overlooked, it is proper to point it out in a sentence or so. Do not compliment the board on the thoroughness of their examination -- they have been sketchy, and you know it. If you wish, merely say, "No thank you, I have nothing further to add." This is a point where you can "talk yourself out" of a good impression or fail to present an important bit of information. Remember, *you close the interview yourself*.

The chairman will then say, "That is all, Mr. _____, thank you." Do not be startled; the interview is over, and quicker than you think. Thank him, gather your belongings and take your leave. Save your sigh of relief for the other side of the door.

How to put your best foot forward

Throughout this entire process, you may feel that the board individually and collectively is trying to pierce your defenses, seek out your hidden weaknesses and embarrass and confuse you. Actually, this is not true. They are obliged to make an appraisal of your qualifications for the job you are seeking, and they want to see you in your best light. Remember, they must interview all candidates and a non-cooperative candidate may become a failure in spite of their best efforts to bring out his qualifications. Here are 15 suggestions that will help you:

1) Be natural – Keep your attitude confident, not cocky

If you are not confident that you can do the job, do not expect the board to be. Do not apologize for your weaknesses, try to bring out your strong points. The board is interested in a positive, not negative, presentation. Cockiness will antagonize any board member and make him wonder if you are covering up a weakness by a false show of strength.

2) Get comfortable, but don't lounge or sprawl

Sit erectly but not stiffly. A careless posture may lead the board to conclude that you are careless in other things, or at least that you are not impressed by the importance of the occasion. Either conclusion is natural, even if incorrect. Do not fuss with your clothing, a pencil or an ashtray. Your hands may occasionally be useful to emphasize a point; do not let them become a point of distraction.

3) Do not wisecrack or make small talk

This is a serious situation, and your attitude should show that you consider it as such. Further, the time of the board is limited – they do not want to waste it, and neither should you.

4) Do not exaggerate your experience or abilities
   In the first place, from information in the application or other interviews and sources, the board may know more about you than you think. Secondly, you probably will not get away with it. An experienced board is rather adept at spotting such a situation, so do not take the chance.

5) If you know a board member, do not make a point of it, yet do not hide it
   Certainly you are not fooling him, and probably not the other members of the board. Do not try to take advantage of your acquaintanceship – it will probably do you little good.

6) Do not dominate the interview
   Let the board do that. They will give you the clues – do not assume that you have to do all the talking. Realize that the board has a number of questions to ask you, and do not try to take up all the interview time by showing off your extensive knowledge of the answer to the first one.

7) Be attentive
   You only have 20 minutes or so, and you should keep your attention at its sharpest throughout. When a member is addressing a problem or question to you, give him your undivided attention. Address your reply principally to him, but do not exclude the other board members.

8) Do not interrupt
   A board member may be stating a problem for you to analyze. He will ask you a question when the time comes. Let him state the problem, and wait for the question.

9) Make sure you understand the question
   Do not try to answer until you are sure what the question is. If it is not clear, restate it in your own words or ask the board member to clarify it for you. However, do not haggle about minor elements.

10) Reply promptly but not hastily
   A common entry on oral board rating sheets is "candidate responded readily," or "candidate hesitated in replies." Respond as promptly and quickly as you can, but do not jump to a hasty, ill-considered answer.

11) Do not be peremptory in your answers
   A brief answer is proper – but do not fire your answer back. That is a losing game from your point of view. The board member can probably ask questions much faster than you can answer them.

12) Do not try to create the answer you think the board member wants
   He is interested in what kind of mind you have and how it works – not in playing games. Furthermore, he can usually spot this practice and will actually grade you down on it.

13) Do not switch sides in your reply merely to agree with a board member
   Frequently, a member will take a contrary position merely to draw you out and to see if you are willing and able to defend your point of view. Do not start a debate, yet do not surrender a good position. If a position is worth taking, it is worth defending.

14) Do not be afraid to admit an error in judgment if you are shown to be wrong

The board knows that you are forced to reply without any opportunity for careful consideration. Your answer may be demonstrably wrong. If so, admit it and get on with the interview.

15) Do not dwell at length on your present job

The opening question may relate to your present assignment. Answer the question but do not go into an extended discussion. You are being examined for a *new* job, not your present one. As a matter of fact, try to phrase ALL your answers in terms of the job for which you are being examined.

Basis of Rating

Probably you will forget most of these "do's" and "don'ts" when you walk into the oral interview room. Even remembering them all will not ensure you a passing grade. Perhaps you did not have the qualifications in the first place. But remembering them will help you to put your best foot forward, without treading on the toes of the board members.

Rumor and popular opinion to the contrary notwithstanding, an oral board wants you to make the best appearance possible. They know you are under pressure – but they also want to see how you respond to it as a guide to what your reaction would be under the pressures of the job you seek. They will be influenced by the degree of poise you display, the personal traits you show and the manner in which you respond.

ABOUT THIS BOOK

This book contains tests divided into Examination Sections. Go through each test, answering every question in the margin. We have also attached a sample answer sheet at the back of the book that can be removed and used. At the end of each test look at the answer key and check your answers. On the ones you got wrong, look at the right answer choice and learn. Do not fill in the answers first. Do not memorize the questions and answers, but understand the answer and principles involved. On your test, the questions will likely be different from the samples. Questions are changed and new ones added. If you understand these past questions you should have success with any changes that arise. Tests may consist of several types of questions. We have additional books on each subject should more study be advisable or necessary for you. Finally, the more you study, the better prepared you will be. This book is intended to be the last thing you study before you walk into the examination room. Prior study of relevant texts is also recommended. NLC publishes some of these in our Fundamental Series. Knowledge and good sense are important factors in passing your exam. Good luck also helps. So now study this Passbook, absorb the material contained within and take that knowledge into the examination. Then do your best to pass that exam.

EXAMINATION SECTION

EXAMINATION SECTION
TEST 1

DIRECTIONS: Each question or incomplete statement is followed by several suggested answers or completions. Select the one that BEST answers the question or completes the statement. *PRINT THE LETTER OF THE CORRECT ANSWER IN THE SPACE AT THE RIGHT.*

1. The one of the following which is the BEST reason for a medical social worker's having a sound foundation of medical information is that she may be able to

    A. determine the degree of disability which each illness may cause
    B. assist the doctors in bringing about solutions to medical problems
    C. instruct visiting nurses in case work
    D. instruct patients in the proper way to carry out medical recommendations
    E. work intelligently as a member of the medical team in helping sick people make the best use of medical care

2. The one of the following which a medical social worker should consider the LEAST desirable during the course of the treatment interview with the client is to

    A. foster a totally dependent attitude
    B. respect the client's judgment
    C. permit the client to talk about possible solutions
    D. respect the client as an individual person
    E. clear the air and let the client talk

3. The one of the following which is MOST likely to be the medical social worker's role with a clinic patient who has a mild case of diabetes is to

    A. help the patient change his environment
    B. help the patient accept his illness
    C. arrange for the placement of his children
    D. arrange for blood sugar tests
    E. arrange convalescent care

4. The one of the following which is the PRIMARY purpose of the teaching of medical students by a medical social worker is to

    A. impress upon them the responsibilities of the medical social worker
    B. increase the number of referrals to the medical social worker
    C. make them aware of the social and emotional factors which may complicate the care of patients
    D. describe the development of social work to them
    E. teach them medical social casework

5. The one of the following functions which is agreed by medical social work authorities to be the PROPER focus of a modern medical social service department is

    A. teaching social aspects of medicine
    B. assisting in research
    C. providing medical relief
    D. completing brief service cases
    E. performing casework

1

6. Medical social work authorities consider a 100% review of a diagnostic group in a hospital an appropriate activity of a medical social worker under certain circumstances PROVIDED the purpose is

   A. individualization
   B. health education
   C. transference
   D. steering
   E. medical follow-up

7. In addition to basic knowledge of social work, the one of the following in which medical social workers are expected to have SPECIAL ability is

   A. recognizing the symptoms of early illness
   B. first aid
   C. follow-up of tuberculosis contacts
   D. working in a team-work relationship with other professions in a medical agency
   E. planning recreation programs in hospital wards

8. The administrator of a hospital is responsible for the total functioning of the institution, and each department head is responsible to the administrator for the proper functioning of his department. Assuming that you are a medical social worker in the hospital and a student nurse is extremely insolent to you or to a patient in your presence, the one of the following to whom you should report her action is

   A. the doctor on service
   B. the director of nurses
   C. your immediate supervisor
   D. the registered nurse on the floor
   E. the hospital administrator

9. An acutely ill mother of a healthy two-week old infant girl is admitted to a hospital at night. The following morning, the husband of the patient phones the medical social worker on the service and demands to know why the baby was refused readmission to the hospital nursery when it only left there the week before.
   The one of the following replies which the medical social worker SHOULD give to the husband is that

   A. there are no vacant bassinets in the nursery
   B. the baby was not admitted to the nursery because she is not sick
   C. if social service had been on duty, the baby would have been admitted
   D. he should report the matter to the medical superintendent
   E. infants are never admitted to the nursery from outside the hospital

10. The one of the following which is the PRIMARY role of social casework is to

    A. direct people who have little knowledge of life toward more satisfying experiences
    B. readjust environmental factors which are hindering a person's social adjustment
    C. help people recognize and handle problems which are not beyond their capacity to solve
    D. give sympathetic understanding to individuals who have social problems
    E. refer individuals to the proper community resource to meet their needs

11. The one of the following which is the PRIME requisite of a good social worker is a   11.____

    A. respect for the worth of an individual
    B. high degree of intelligence
    C. knowledge of psychiatry and mental hygiene
    D. sound knowledge of resources
    E. good knowledge of human behavior

12. Of the following, the one which is the BEST definition of social casework is   12.____

    A. a substitute for proper family relations
    B. a treatment process for sick persons
    C. a method of mass treatment of social problems
    D. an individual approach to people in trouble
    E. a method of solving financial problems

13. The one of the following which may be said to have come FIRST in the history and development of social work as a profession is   13.____

    A. analytical assistance
    B. friendly visiting by volunteer workers
    C. psychological approach
    D. outdoor relief
    E. social diagnoses

14. The one of the following circumstances in which casework service would be MOST likely to bring about a *successful* solution is in a situation in which   14.____

    A. a family is satisfied with things as they are
    B. the attitudes and habits of a patient are firmly entrenched and of long standing
    C. for one reason or another, there is only financial need
    D. the worker is working for the community against the desires of the patient
    E. a family seeks help with the problem of an adolescent child

15. The one of the following which is an IDEAL social casework situation is a(n)   15.____

    A. prisoner released from a reformatory who is very penitent for his crime
    B. person who is pronounced cured of congenital syphilis
    C. unwed mother who is seeking assistance by court action to punish the putative father
    D. psychoneurotic patient who is aware that her problems come from within her environment and her reaction to this environment
    E. person who knows he needs help, is capable of cooperating, and seeks some solution to his problem

16. In distinguishing between functions of a public agency and a private agency, the one of the following functions which would MOST likely belong only to a private agency is to   16.____

    A. investigate occupational resources
    B. investigate need for complete financial assistance
    C. evaluate need of an individual for rehabilitation
    D. do casework with the marginal income group
    E. determine budgetary needs of the indigent group

17. The one of the following services to patients which is not considered as legitimately falling within the functions of the medical social service department of a hospital is the

    A. securing of appliances
    B. arranging for convalescent care
    C. arranging for day care for children
    D. dispensing of medications
    E. reporting to community agencies

18. A voluntary hospital is a hospital

    A. in which doctors are forbidden to accept fees
    B. which accepts only patients unable to pay the full cost of their care
    C. which is entirely supported by public contributions
    D. in which most of the hospital workers are volunteers
    E. which is a non-profit institution

19. The one of the following which is a TRUE statement regarding the commissioner of hospitals is that he is

    A. responsible for the health of all residents of the city
    B. appointed by the mayor
    C. required to sign all commitment papers
    D. responsible only to the governor of the state
    E. an elected official for a two-year term

20. The one of the following which is a TRUE statement is that medical care in a tax-supported hospital is available to

    A. only those who have settlement in the area
    B. only those receiving public assistance
    C. all persons in need of medical treatment
    D. emergency cases only
    E. persons with contagious diseases only

21. The one of the following which is the PRIMARY function of the department of health is

    A. the treatment of contagious diseases
    B. education of the public towards better health
    C. conducting statistical research in problems of health
    D. providing nursing service to the indigent
    E. the distribution of health literature

22. A premarital blood test is required prior to the issuance of a marriage license. This requirement may be waived when

    A. both parties have been married before to different spouses
    B. the woman is pregnant at the time the marriage license is requested
    C. both parties have had physical examinations by a private physician
    D. both parties present reports of negative blood tests taken 6 months prior to the request for a license
    E. the man is over 65 years of age and in apparent good health

23. The one of the following statements regarding the care and treatment of tuberculous patients in the state which is FALSE is: 23.____

   A. If it is established that an alien was suffering from tuberculosis at the time of landing or becomes a public charge as a result of this condition within five years, he is eligible for sanitarium care for a one-year period in a federal hospital
   B. Any person affected with a communicable disease such as tuberculosis, likely to be dangerous to the lives and health of other persons, may be removed to a hospital designated by a board of health, upon the report of a duly authorized physician
   C. Care and treatment provided by the state or by any county or city for persons suffering from tuberculosis shall be available without cost or charge to any person having state residence and at the discretion of the state commissioner of health to any other person in the state who is suffering from tuberculosis
   D. Persons approved for admission to state hospitals unable to pay for transportation may be furnished such transportation by the superintendent of the hospital, and that transportation to another hospital for special care and treatment may also be furnished
   E. Any person who volunteers to assume and pay for the cost of the care and treatment of a patient suffering from tuberculosis shall be permitted to do so, but no state, county, city, or other public official shall request or require such payment

24. The one of the following which forms a PRIMARY aim of school child guidance clinics is the 24.____

   A. treatment of the parents
   B. prevention of juvenile delinquency
   C. prevention of mental ill health
   D. prevention of truancy
   E. treatment of the narcotic addict

25. The Community Chest and the Council of Social Agencies in cities where both exist work cooperatively to provide the greatest welfare for the entire community. The one of the following functions which would fall EXCLUSIVELY within the functions of the Community Chest is to 25.____

   A. give group work service to the community
   B. provide recreational facilities to members
   C. support agency functions and programs
   D. raise funds for the social welfare and health agencies
   E. interpret the work of individual agencies

26. The one of the following which is the PRIMARY function of the Tuberculosis and Health Association is 26.____

   A. psychometric testing
   B. convalescent care
   C. education of the public
   D. financial assistance
   E. surgical treatment

27. The one of the following which is the CHIEF purpose of the visits paid by a public health nurse to a patient in his home is to

    A. educate patient or patient group to give adequate care
    B. make epidemiological investigations
    C. report to the truant authority
    D. give reassurance to patient and patient group
    E. evaluate the home situation for emotional and physical strains

28. When a post-partum patient and her baby are discharged after a week in a hospital and the case is referred to the Visiting Nurse Service, the one of the following which is the USUAL routine for the visiting nurse is to

    A. visit daily for the next week to check on the mother's condition and to bathe the baby
    B. arrange for housekeeping service if it seems necessary
    C. keep in touch with the nurse in the school attended by other children in the family to avoid exposing the baby to a communicable disease
    D. keep the referral on file unless the patient is under a physician's care at home
    E. visit within a short time of the patient's return home to instruct her in the care of the baby

29. A 35-year-old woman who had always lived in New York City was diagnosed as having osteomyelitis of the left tibia, and was admitted to a New York City hospital for treatment. Conservative treatment was of no avail, and she had an amputation below the left knee. The medical social worker was called in to see her as she said she had spent five months in San Francisco, California, just prior to her hospitalization and had no means of support. She needed an artificial leg before leaving the hospital, plus financial support. Before her illness, she was a typist.
    The one of the following agencies which should be contacted FIRST is the

    A. New York State Department of Social Services
    B. California State Department of Welfare
    C. New York State Division of Vocational Rehabilitation
    D. Welfare Council of New York City
    E. Rehabilitation Division of the New York City Department of Hospitals

30. When the woman described in the preceding question was ready to leave the hospital and the medical social worker was seeking financial support for maintenance, the one of the following agencies which SHOULD be contacted is the

    A. Department of Social Services
    B. Florence Crittenton League
    C. Division of Placement and Unemployment Insurance
    D. Workmen's Compensation Office
    E. Community Service Society

31. The name of the following institutions which is NOT under the management and control of the State Department of Correction is the   31._____

    A. Berkshire Industrial Farm
    B. Wallkill Prison
    C. Woodbourne Correctional Institution
    D. Elmira Reformatory
    E. State Vocational Institution

32. The one of the following which can be considered the PRIMARY purpose of the Social Security Act is the   32._____

    A. insurance against loss of earnings by an injured employee
    B. furthering of the security of the citizen and his family through social insurance
    C. distribution of surplus wealth among the needy classes
    D. development of an economic balance between the wealthy and the poor
    E. insurance of dependents against need

33. The passage of the Social Security Act in 1935 points toward the establishment of a broad national welfare program. The one of the following ways in which federal funds are provided, according to the provisions of the Act, is through   33._____

    A. payment of all the administrative funds used in disbursing state and local funds
    B. maintenance of adequate institutions to foster a good national program
    C. lump sum payments to all needy blind and widows
    D. part payment in participation with state and local funds
    E. full payment to individual recipients

34. The one of the following groups of persons which is ELIGIBLE for benefits under the Social Security Act is   34._____

    A. persons who have worked a required period of time in certain covered occupations
    B. the dependents of workmen injured or killed while on the job
    C. all those over 65 years old who are unable to find employment
    D. the dependents of soldiers, sailors, or marines killed while on combat duty
    E. all citizens who have reached the age of 65 years, whether or not in need of financial assistance

35. Of the following categories, the one which was MOST recently added to those which are covered under the Social Security Act is   35._____

    A. the blind   B. the permanently disabled
    C. crippled adults   D. the aged
    E. dependent children

KEY (CORRECT ANSWERS)

1. E	11. A	21. B	31. A
2. A	12. D	22. B	32. B
3. B	13. B	23. A	33. D
4. C	14. E	24. C	34. A
5. E	15. E	25. D	35. B
6. A	16. D	26. C	
7. D	17. D	27. A	
8. C	18. E	28. E	
9. E	19. B	29. C	
10. C	20. C	30. A	

EXAMINATION SECTION
TEST 1

DIRECTIONS: Each question or incomplete statement is followed by several suggested answers or completions. Select the one that BEST answers the question or completes the statement. *PRINT THE LETTER OF THE CORRECT ANSWER IN THE SPACE AT THE RIGHT.*

1. The one of the following diseases which is the LEADING cause of death in the 10-to-15 year age group is 1.____
   - A. cancer
   - B. tuberculosis
   - C. poliomyelitis
   - D. diabetes
   - E. rheumatic fever

2. The one of the following which would MOST likely be a result of untreated syphilis is 2.____
   - A. paresis
   - B. phlebitis
   - C. carcinoma
   - D. silicosis
   - E. angina pectoris

3. The one of the following which is MOST likely to be used in establishing a diagnosis of epilepsy is a(n) 3.____
   - A. electrocardiogram
   - B. spinal x-ray
   - C. fluoroscopic examination
   - D. electroencephalogram
   - E. psychometric examination

4. The pathology of diabetes involves the FAILURE of the body to produce an adequate supply of 4.____
   - A. sugar
   - B. carbohydrates
   - C. insulin
   - D. salt
   - E. bile

5. The one of the following statements that is TRUE about diabetes is that 5.____
   - A. it can generally be cured if medical orders are followed
   - B. it can generally be kept under control but not cured
   - C. it is an infectious disease
   - D. blindness is an inevitable result of it
   - E. controlled diabetes is a progressively disabling disease

6. Scurvy is caused by a deficiency of vitamin 6.____
   - A. A
   - B. B
   - C. C
   - D. E
   - E. K

7. Vitamin D deficiency is common because 7.____
   - A. it can only be injected
   - B. it is generally associated with poorly tasting foods
   - C. only physicians can administer it
   - D. it is not found naturally in many foods

8. The one of the following vitamins that is used as an aid in coagulating blood is vitamin 8.____
   - A. A
   - B. B
   - C. C
   - D. E
   - E. K

2 (#1)

9. The one of the following statements that is TRUE of Duchenne muscular dystrophy is that
   A. it is transmitted to the male children through the mother
   B. the male is the carrier of the disease
   C. the brain is primarily affected because of a lack of blood supply
   D. it is caused by a nutritional deficiency in the antepartum period
   E. only female children are susceptible to the disease

9.____

10. If a patient is repeatedly admitted to the hospital because of a series of mishaps in which he has suffered broken bones, the one of the following that is MOST likely to be true is that he is
    A. a rigid person   B. a diabetic   C. malingering
    D. accident prone   E. psychotic

10.____

11. The one of the following groups of illnesses that is known to be caused by bacteria is
    A. mental diseases   B. acute infectious diseases
    C. nutritional diseases   D. degenerative diseases
    E. cancerous tumors

11.____

12. The one of the following with which Hodgkin's Disease is COMMONLY associated is
    A. neurasthenia   B. meningitis   C. poliomyelitis
    D. cancer   E. tuberculosis

12.____

13. The one of the following diseases in which the determination of the sedimentation rate is IMPORTANT for diagnostic purposes is
    A. rheumatic heart disease   B. congenital heart disease
    C. hypertensive heart disease D. diabetes
    E. gonorrhea

13.____

14. The one of the following disease classifications that would INCLUDE spinal meningitis is
    A. cancer or tumor   B. nutritional disease
    C. acute infectious disease   D. focal or local infection
    E. acute poisoning or intoxication

14.____

15. The one of the following diseases that may cause visual impairment and blindness is
    A. ringworm   B. osteomyelitis
    C. poliomyelitis   D. gall bladder disease
    E. diabetes

15.____

16. The one of the following that is NOT an anesthetic is
    A. cholesterol   B. nitrous oxide   C. sodium pentothal
    D. procaine   E. ethyl chloride

16.____

17. The one of the following that BEST describes the restrictions to be applied to Mr. K., a cardiac patient classified, according to the standards of the American Heart Association, as functional, Class IVD, is
    A. limited activity
    B. complete bed rest
    C. four hours rest daily
    D. prohibition of stair climbing, alcohol or tobacco
    E. convalescent status

18. Over time, geriatrics has become an increasingly important branch of medicine CHIEFLY due to
    A. greater specialization within the medical profession
    B. the discovery of penicillin and aureomycin
    C. advances in medical education
    D. increases in hospitalization
    E. the increase in the span of life

19. The one of the following which is MOST likely to be an occupational disease is
    A. cancer
    B. cerebral hemorrhage
    C. septicemia
    D. asthma
    E. nephritis

20. The one of the following that is a NUTRITIONAL disease is
    A. tuberculosis
    B. scurvy
    C. hepatitis
    D. lymphoma
    E. scabies

21. Morbidity rate refers to the
    A. incidence of an illness
    B. ratio of births to deaths
    C. bacterial count
    D. degree of disability caused by an illness
    E. death rate

22. A pediatrician is a doctor who specializes in the treatment of
    A. children
    B. foot diseases
    C. disabling illnesses
    D. orthopedic diseases
    E. the aged

23. A sadistic person is one who
    A. receives gratification through suffering pain
    B. secures a great deal of satisfaction from his own body
    C. receives gratification from inflicting pain on others
    D. turns all feelings towards others back into his own personality
    E. seeks solace through deep mental depression

24. The one of the following which is said to be the masculine counterpart of the *Electra Complex* is the _____ complex.
    A. sexual perversion
    B. frustration
    C. Oedipus
    D. reanimation
    E. repression

25. The one of the following conditions for which a patient would be admitted to a state mental hospital is
    A. schizophrenia
    B. muscular dystrophy
    C. pathological lying
    D. congenital syphilis
    E. psychoneurosis

25.____

26. The one of the following statements which BEST describes the difference between a hallucination and a delusion is that
    A. hallucinations occur only at night
    B. delusions occur only with menopause
    C. delusions are primarily provoked by sexual function
    D. a hallucination has a basis in beliefs or ideas
    E. a delusion has a basis in beliefs or ideas

26.____

27. Finger sucking in early childhood has long been a subject of discussion among psychiatrists.
    The one of the following statements that is GENERALLY accepted as true is that
    A. finger sucking denotes pending neuroses and the parents need psychiatric consultation
    B. finger sucking is a normal activity of early childhood and should not be interfered with
    C. finger sucking alters the child's facial contours and should be heavily discouraged
    D. finger sucking by a child over nine months old is due to emotional upset and needs treatment
    E. the physician should discuss possible remedial measures such as guards on fingers

27.____

28. The one of the following who is said to be the *Father of Medicine* is
    A. Hippocrates
    B. Pasteur
    C. Galen
    D. Sydenham
    E. Plato

28.____

29. The one of the following who is credited with the improvement of conditions in mental hospitals and the founding of new ones in the United States is
    A. Andrew Jackson
    B. Dorothea Dix
    C. William Knowlton
    D. Robert Stack
    E. Rene Laennec

29.____

30. The one of the following doctors whose name is COMMONLY associated with much of the early growth and subsequent progress of medical social work is Dr.
    A. Sigmund Freud
    B. Richard C. Cabot
    C. Elizabeth Blackwell
    D. Carmyn Lombardo
    E. Thomas Parran

30.____

KEY (CORRECT ANSWERS)

1.	A	11.	B	21.	A
2.	A	12.	D	22.	A
3.	D	13.	A	23.	C
4.	C	14.	C	24.	C
5.	B	15.	E	25.	A
6.	C	16.	A	26.	E
7.	D	17.	B	27.	B
8.	E	18.	E	28.	A
9.	A	19.	D	29.	B
10.	D	20.	B	30.	B

EXAMINATION SECTION
TEST 1

DIRECTIONS: Each question or incomplete statement is followed by several suggested answers or completions. Select the one that BEST answers the question or completes the statement. *PRINT THE LETTER OF THE CORRECT ANSWER IN THE SPACE AT THE RIGHT.*

1. Social case work is PRIMARILY 1.____

    A. a method of preventing juvenile delinquency
    B. the art of listening to others
    C. an interpretation to lay persons of social problems
    D. the determination of the individual's ability to meet situations
    E. an individual approach to people in trouble

2. Statistics show that the MAJORITY of people *initially* go to social agencies for 2.____

    A. recreational purposes
    B. help with financial problems
    C. vocational guidance
    D. help with marital problems
    E. help with emotional problems

3. Of the following, the trend followed by public welfare agencies at the present time is to 3.____

    A. give *relief in kind* to avoid wasteful spending of money
    B. give food and clothing vouchers on short–term cases
    C. discourage work relief projects
    D. give *cash relief* where the financial need has been established
    E. make public lists of relief recipients

4. In the initial interview with a client, the one of the following which is the MOST important is for the medical social worker to 4.____

    A. establish a sound social diagnosis
    B. outline the functions of her agency
    C. be aware of treatment possibilities
    D. listen closely and plan treatment
    E. determine what the client sees as the problem

5. The one of the following which is the PRIMARY function of a medical social consultant in a family welfare agency is to 5.____

    A. carry a case load of families having medical problems
    B. interpret the medical diagnoses to the clients
    C. confer directly with doctors concerning the clients' medical needs
    D. study the health needs of the families
    E. assist the case workers in the handling of medical problems

6. The one of the following which is the PRIMARY function of the family welfare agency is to

   A. provide convalescent care for sick children
   B. establish need and eligibility for proper housing for low income families in order to meet minimum health standards
   C. supervise family relations, thereby insuring the welfare and prevention of delinquency of children
   D. offer vocational rehabilitation services and encourage employment of the handicapped person
   E. help individuals and families meet problems and make the best possible adjustment within their limitations

7. The one of the following social workers who is well–known for her work in social diagnosis is

   A. Bertha Reynolds
   B. Janet Thornton
   C. Antoinette Cannon
   D. Harriet Bartlett
   E. Mabel McGuire

8. The one of the following which is the PRIMARY function of the social service exchange is to

   A. distinguish the frauds from the needy cases in almsgiving
   B. promote more efficient service to individuals
   C. discourage professional begging through the recording system
   D. insure a fair distribution of welfare funds to agencies
   E. distinguish worthy from unworthy families prior to giving assistance

9. The one of the following which is NOT considered a function of the private family agency is the

   A. rehabilitation of the handicapped through *sheltered employment*
   B. planning of summer camp placements for underprivileged children
   C. assisting of unwed mothers in planning for adoption of their babies
   D. giving of consultant and referral service for the indigent
   E. giving of supplemental financial assistance to marginal income families

10. The author of SOCIAL WORK RECORDING is

    A. Grace White
    B. Bertha Reynolds
    C. Gordon Hamilton
    D. Richard Cabot
    E. Carol Cooley

11. The one of the following functions which should NEVER be assumed by a medical social worker in a hospital is

    A. planning convalescent care for private patients
    B. routine social review for certain groups
    C. accepting surrenders of babies for adoption
    D. social admitting of indigent patients
    E. terminal care planning, if necessary

12. The one of the following which is the PRIMARY responsibility of any hospital is to

    A. keep adequate records on all patients
    B. train the medical staff adequately
    C. assist in the advancement of medical knowledge
    D. render care to the sick and injured
    E. promote community health and wellbeing

13. As the medical social worker in a hospital, you have submitted the necessary forms to the Department of Social Services for a prenatal patient to be granted elastic stockings because of severe varicosities. After four weeks have elapsed, the patient reports that she has not received the stockings.
    The one of the following procedures which you should follow is to

    A. call the social investigator on the case
    B. notify the investigato's supervisor
    C. tell the patient that such matters take a long time
    D. purchase stockings through hospital funds
    E. call the appropriate medical social worker at the Department of Social Services

14. The one of the following which is the PRIMARY function of the social case work supervisor in a hospital setting is to

    A. act as a liaison between the administration and the workers
    B. assist and teach her workers to do their job adequately
    C. teach workers, doctors, and nurses the value of case work
    D. administer the expenditures of funds
    E. determine policies of the department as they affect the hospital

15. Assume that as the medical social worker in a hospital, you are called to the accident ward. The doctor states that the unconscious woman on the table has had a miscarriage and it will be necessary to admit her for a curettage. Her four children, age 6, 4, 3, and 2, are in the waiting room of the hospital. Police report that there are no relatives at the address given.
    The one of the following which should be your FIRST step in the case is to

    A. clear the case with social service exchange
    B. call the child care division of the Department of Social Services
    C. arrange for homemaker service
    D. place the children in an emergency shelter
    E. take the children to the Speedwell Society

16. A patient in a voluntary hospital dispensary is in need of a regular supply of bandages and sterile dressings because of a diagnosis of incurable cancer. The patient's family who has been supporting him is unable to meet this additional expense.
The one of the following which would be the BEST procedure for the medical social worker in the hospital to follow is to

    A. send the patient to a city hospital which by law must provide dressings
    B. obtain the necessary form from the Department of Social Services to authorize the hospital pharmacy to dispense these articles
    C. advise the patient to make bandages and sterile dressings
    D. send an order in duplicate for these to the Department of Social Services
    E. contact the local chapter of the American Cancer Society

17. Suppose that a patient in a voluntary hospital is to be transferred to a nursing home in another borough of the city. She has no funds to pay for transportation by an ambulance. Of the following, transfer by ambulance should be arranged through the

    A. Department of Hospitals
    B. Social Service Department of a private hospital
    C. Department of Health
    D. Department of Social Services
    E. Shut-In Society

18. The one of the following statements which is TRUE in regard to the voluntary, non-profit hospitals is that

    A. they are exempt from paying taxes
    B. patients must subject themselves for research purposes
    C. payments may be made only for the exact cost of medical care
    D. the Department of Health has no control over them
    E. no doctor may receive compensation for services rendered

19. Of the following, the CHIEF value of the medical social worker's attendance at ward rounds and conferences with the doctors on service is that

    A. knowledge of medical matters gives security to the worker
    B. the social and medical planning can be coordinated
    C. the worker can report verbally to the doctor rather than dictate extensive records
    D. the patient sees the worker as a part of the medical team
    E. the doctors find it convenient to make referrals at that time

20. The one of the following to whom the director of the social service department of a voluntary hospital is generally responsible is the

    A. United Hospital Fund
    B. board of managers
    C. director of nurses
    D. hospital administrator
    E. medical advisory committee

21. Volunteers can be an asset in the functioning of any hospital. 21.____
The one of the following which represents their GREATEST value to the hospital from the point of view of public relations is

    A. interpreting the hospital to the community
    B. popularizing the hospital with the patients by meeting their personal needs
    C. replacing employees during the labor shortage
    D. lowering the cost of caring for the sick
    E. giving service to visiting relatives which might not otherwise be available

22. The one of the following hospitals which is operated by the Department of Hospitals is 22.____

    A. the Hospital for Joint Diseases
    B. Columbus Hospital
    C. Gouverneur Hospital
    D. Brooklyn Thoracic Hospital
    E. Montefiore Hospital

23. Assume that you are the medical social worker in a clinic. A patient complains to you 23.____
about the time involved in clinic attendance, questioning particularly the need for repeated clinic visits prior to his being given treatment recommendations.
The one of the following you should do FIRST is to

    A. explain that the doctors give their time free, and patience is necessary
    B. interpret the needs of each patient who is waiting at the clinic at the time
    C. describe the overcrowding and the need for better community resources
    D. interpret the possible necessity of laboratory procedures prior to accurate diagnosis and treatment measures
    E. discuss the length of time involved in visiting a private doctor during his office hours

24. If a forty-year-old woman with severe rheumatic heart disease requests her doctor to 24.____
sterilize her by a tubal ligation, he may do so legally PROVIDED he

    A. can testify that further pregnancies would be dangerous
    B. has the consent of the woman with two witnesses present
    C. has the signed consent of the woman and her husband
    D. explains the nature of the operation to the woman and her husband
    E. has a court order to perform the operation

25. In regard to the care of the chronically ill, the one of the following which is recommended 25.____
CHIEFLY is the

    A. establishment of more chronic hospitals specifically designated as caring only for the chronically ill
    B. establishment of more hospital facilities for their care in the community general hospitals
    C. placing of greater responsibility for their care upon relatives and friends
    D. payment of larger fees to the privately owned nursing homes
    E. conduct of research into the causes of chronic illness by a greater number of voluntary hospitals

KEY (CORRECT ANSWERS)

1.	E	11.	C
2.	B	12.	D
3.	D	13.	E
4.	E	14.	B
5.	E	15.	B
6.	E	16.	E
7.	A	17.	A
8.	B	18.	A
9.	E	19.	B
10.	C	20.	D

21. A
22. C
23. D
24. C
25. B

TEST 2

DIRECTIONS: Each question or incomplete statement is followed by several suggested answers or completions. Select the one that BEST answers the question or completes the statement. *PRINT THE LETTER OF THE CORRECT ANSWER IN THE SPACE AT THE RIGHT.*

1. It is important for a medical social worker to have a basic knowledge of medical information MAINLY because 1.____

    A. in working with the doctor she must prove her competence
    B. patients will ask pertinent questions regarding diagnosis and treatment of their illnesses
    C. she can encourage patients to maintain good health standards
    D. the social problems of the patients may vary according to the nature of their illnesses
    E. she can help patients to avoid the major illnesses

2. In order to be admitted to a state tuberculosis sanitarium, the patient MUST 2.____

    A. be diagnosed as an active tuberculosis case
    B. be unable to pay for private care
    C. have legal residence in the state
    D. apply for admission through the division of handicapped
    E. commit himself

3. The one of the following which is the PRIMARY aim of public health programs in relation to illness and disease is to 3.____

    A. cure   B. palliate
    C. prevent   D. conduct research
    E. ameliorate

4. Every child before admission to school is required to be vaccinated against 4.____

    A. smallpox   B. diphtheria   C. typhoid
    D. scarlet fever   E. whooping cough

5. Cancer is considered a public health responsibility MAINLY because of the 5.____

    A. enormity of the problem
    B. lack of adequate diagnostic facilities
    C. need for research
    D. familial disposition
    E. value of contact examination

6. The one of the following whom the U.S. Children's Bureau would NOT consider a crippled or a handicapped child is a child with 6.____

    A. cerebral palsy   B. nephrosis
    C. poliomyelitis   D. a cardiac disorder
    E. a club foot

7. The one of the following which is the PRIMARY function of the American Heart Association is

   A. fundraising for indigent patients
   B. promotion of research
   C. provision of convalescent facilities
   D. education of the public
   E. supervision of heart clinics

8. The one of the following which is NOT a function of the visiting nurse organizations is

   A. relief of the sick in their homes
   B. giving injections to patients at home
   C. supervising health care of the newborn at home
   D. education of the patient group to give adequate care to the patient
   E. full-time bedside nursing care in the home

9. The father of a man in the armed forces became seriously ill and was hospitalized in a critical condition. He kept calling for his son, who was stationed in this country. The one of the following you would call in order to ask that the son be granted a leave to see his father is the

   A. American Legion   B. son's commanding officer
   C. Veterans Administration   D. Traveler's Aid Society
   E. American Red Cross

10. The one of the following which is a convalescent home for the care of cardiac patients with rheumatic fever is

    A. Elizabeth House   B. Eleanora's Home
    C. Francis Sanatorium   D. Charles Hospital
    E. Giles' Home

11. The one of the following which BEST describes the Welfare Council is:

    A. A council of agencies to decide upon the functioning of each member agency
    B. A group of lay persons whose function is to insure good welfare practices
    C. A council of wealthy citizens, with one paid employee, to give informational service
    D. A council of social agencies to coordinate existing welfare services
    E. The central channel for the collection and distribution of welfare funds

12. The one of the following agencies which is NOT a settlement house is the

    A. Hudson Guild   B. House of St. Giles
    C. Casita Maria   D. Greenwich House
    E. Hartley House

13. The one of the following circumstances which will warrant a 'home teacher' for a child registered in a grammar school is if   13.____

    A. he is registered in a public school
    B. he will be unable to attend regular school for at least a month
    C. he has been known to suffer from a lack of schooling
    D. his family is agreeable to the plan and will cooperate
    E. his intelligence quotient demonstrates he will benefit by this

14. In order to have a child admitted to the Willowbrook Hospital, application must be made to the   14.____

    A. City Department of Hospitals
    B. City Department of Health
    C. State Department of Mental Hygiene
    D. State Board of Social Services
    E. City Department of Correction

15. There are no private or voluntary hospitals in the city whose PRIMARY function is the treatment of   15.____

    A. orthopedic diseases
    B. the chronically ill
    C. cancer
    D. nervous diseases
    E. contagious diseases

16. Of the following, those who are legally entitled to special preference when applying for housing through the Housing Authority are   16.____

    A. handicapped persons
    B. persons in the lowest income group
    C. persons in rooming houses
    D. honorably discharged veterans
    E. families with many children

17. The one of the following which is the PRIMARY purpose of the Worker's Compensation Law is to   17.____

    A. protect both the employer and the employee
    B. insure full pay to sick workers
    C. insure favorable work conditions in dangerous positions
    D. eliminate *sweat shop labor* and maintain adequate wages
    E. replace the need for unions in large factories

18. A person whose employment comes within the provisions of the State Unemployment Compensation Act, upon losing his position, is ALWAYS entitled to receive unemployment compensation if he   18.____

    A. is unable to obtain work in his specialized field
    B. applies for compensation within 48 hours of the termination of his employment
    C. has worked in certain occupations for a specific number of quarters in the previous year
    D. is able to prove that he lost his employment through no fault of his own
    E. can prove that his family will be in need until he obtains employment again

19. A legally married woman who has been living continuously with her husband bears a child who she claims is not her husband's child.
The one of the following statements which is TRUE in connection with the placing of this child for legal adoption is that the

   A. alleged father must give his consent for adoption
   B. mother alone is required to give her consent for adoption
   C. child cannot be adopted legally
   D. alleged father must prove the child was his
   E. woman's husband must give his consent for adoption

19.____

20. Many states have passed the so-called disability benefit laws.
The one of the following which is a TRUE statement in connection with these laws is that

   A. cash benefits for occupational injuries or illnesses are paid
   B. the employer must pay all employees half salary when illness occurs
   C. both employees and employers are covered by insurance to meet the cost of their illness
   D. cash benefits are paid to workers who lose wages because of non-occupational illness or accident
   E. the federal government will pay administrative costs of enforcement

20.____

KEY (CORRECT ANSWERS)

1.	D		11.	D
2.	A		12.	B
3.	C		13.	B
4.	A		14.	C
5.	A		15.	E
6.	B		16.	D
7.	D		17.	A
8.	E		18.	C
9.	E		19.	E
10.	C		20.	D

TEST 3

DIRECTIONS: Each question or incomplete statement is followed by several suggested answers or completions. Select the one that BEST answers the question or completes the statement. *PRINT THE LETTER OF THE CORRECT ANSWER IN THE SPACE AT THE RIGHT.*

1. The one of the following which is a TRUE statement about the Social Security Act is that it

    A. provides with a pension everyone who is over 65 years old
    B. ensures financial security for children of aged parents
    C. provides a minimum economic basic security for millions
    D. eliminates poverty under our present economy
    E. provides employment for the older age group

2. The one of the following which was MOST recently added to the categories of federal public assistance is

    A. aid to the permanently disabled
    B. aid to dependent children
    C. aid to the blind
    D. old age assistance
    E. home relief

3. Of the following statements relating to social security, the one which is TRUE is that

    A. a person receiving a monthly social security check may receive supplementary assistance from the Department of Social Services
    B. every person over 65 years of age is entitled to benefits through the Bureau of Old Age and Survivors' Insurance
    C. a person must give positive proof that he is in need and has no relatives to assist him before he is eligible for a social security check
    D. a person who lives in an old age home is not eligible to receive a social security check
    E. a person may receive a social security check while he is working provided he does not earn over $5,000 a year

4. Under the social security laws, a mother with children under 16 years may ALWAYS obtain an Aid to Dependent Children allotment if

    A. her husband is killed in the line of duty in the United States Armed Services
    B. she proves that, due to her husband's illness or death, the family is in financial need
    C. she is widowed and is unable to obtain gainful employment
    D. she has demonstrated that it is necessary for her to remain at home with her children
    E. the husband has deserted the family

5. The one of the following programs which is administered and operated ONLY by the federal government is

   A. services for crippled children
   B. aid to the needy blind
   C. aid to dependent children
   D. old age and survivors' insurance
   E. aid to the permanently disabled

6. Under the Department of Health, Education, and Welfare, there is provision for a federal-state program of vocational rehabilitation.
   The one of the following which is the BASIC objective of the total program is to

   A. prevent disabling diseases
   B. restore disabled persons in body and spirit
   C. provide appliances where necessary
   D. rehabilitate the mentally defective
   E. retrain disabled servicemen

7. The one of the following agencies which administers the U.S. Public Health Service is the

   A. U.S. Children's Bureau
   B. Treasury Department
   C. National Security Resources Board
   D. National Research Council
   E. Department of Health, Education and Welfare

8. The one of the following which historically was the FIRST function of what is now the U.S. Public Health Service is

   A. the provision of medical and hospital care for the nation's merchant seamen
   B. research into the causes of contagious diseases
   C. the establishment of the Pure Food and Drug Act
   D. the provision of care for the mentally disturbed
   E. administration of city and state departments of health

9. The one of the following U.S. Public Health Service hospitals which gives treatment to narcotic addicts is the

   A. Freedmen's Hospital, Washington, D.C.
   B. Carville Hospital, Carville, La.
   C. U.S. Public Health Service Hospital, Lexington, Ky.
   D. U.S. Public Health Service Hospital, Stapleton, S.I., N.Y.
   E. U.S. Public Health Service Hospital, Manhattan Beach, Brooklyn, N.Y.

Questions 10-15.

DIRECTIONS: Questions 10 through 15 are to be answered SOLELY on the basis of the facts given below.

CASE A

A forty-eight-year old single woman who has Parkinson's syndrome comes to the dispensary of a voluntary general hospital for treatment of excessive vaginal bleeding. She is admitted to the hospital as a *City case* after she proves that she is supported by a Department of Social Services allowance. She has been living in a furnished room and has been receiving a restaurant allowance. A biopsy is done, and a diagnosis of advanced carcinoma of the cervix is made. The hospital is not equipped to treat the patient and wishes her transferred to a city hospital for surgery.

10. As a *City case*, the one of the following statements which is TRUE is that

    A. only emergency treatment pending transfer to the city hospital will be rendered
    B. the city will assume the complete cost of any medical care rendered
    C. the patient's welfare checks will be used to pay her hospital expenses
    D. the voluntary hospital will be reimbursed by the city for care given on a per diem basis
    E. as a non-paying patient, she agrees to enter the voluntary hospital for diagnostic and research purposes only

11. Of the following, the BEST definition of biopsy is

    A. an examination of the substance obtained through a gastric lavage
    B. the removal and microscopic examination of a piece of tissue
    C. a laboratory examination of vaginal bleeding
    D. a blood test showing cancer cells in the bloodstream
    E. a fluoroscopic examination of a body organ

12. The one of the following departments which may authorize the transfer of this patient from the voluntary to the city hospital is the

    A. Department of Social Services
    B. Police Department
    C. Department of Health
    D. Department of Hospitals
    E. Department of Investigation

13. If, as the medical social worker in the voluntary hospital, you have known this woman and have been aware of her fear of surgery, the one of the following steps which would be BEST for you to take in order to help her in this transfer to a city hospital is to

    A. tell her that you will call the medical social worker in the city hospital who will help her during her stay there
    B. tell her that you will discuss her fears with the doctor at the city hospital
    C. promise to visit her at the city hospital and keep in touch with her
    D. tell her that the Department of Social Services investigator will visit her at the city hospital
    E. describe to her all the things which will be done during the surgery to allay her fears

14. When the Department of Social Services investigator hears of the patient's illness and hospitalization, the one of the following actions which he should take IMMEDIATELY is to

    A. close the case pending diagnosis
    B. notify the landlord not to hold the room
    C. recall any checks issued within the past ten days
    D. visit the patient in the hospital
    E. telephone the hospital for verification

15. Suppose the patient is to be discharged from the city hospital following surgery, but will need two or three months of nursing home care before she is able to return to living alone in a furnished room.
    The one of the following which will have to finance such nursing home care is the

    A. American Cancer Society
    B. Department of Social Services
    C. Ladies' Auxiliary of the city hospital
    D. patient's relatives or friends
    E. Department of Hospitals

Questions 16-17.

DIRECTIONS: Questions 16 and 17 are to be answered SOLELY on the basis of the facts given below.

CASE B

A 22-year-old pregnant woman was referred to medical social service by the nurse in the clinic of a city hospital. The nurse reported that the patient had cried following the examination which disclosed her pregnancy and, when questioned by the doctor, she said she was very distressed by her marital situation. You, as the medical social worker assigned to the case, learn that her husband is the superintendent of the house in which they live and that he receives free rent but no salary. He does odd jobs to earn money and buys groceries and other necessities, but will not give his wife any money. The husband drinks very heavily.

The patient says this is her second pregnancy. The first child, now 15 months old, was born five months after her marriage. She says she wants to leave her husband but wonders how she can support her babies. She would agree to stay with her husband if he would give her money.

16. On the basis of the facts given in Case B, the one of the following steps you would take is:

    A. Referral to the Department of Social Services
    B. Referral to a family agency
    C. Referral to Domestic Relations Court
    D. Discussion of the problem with the patient's husband
    E. Discussion of the problem with available relatives

17. As the patient described in Case B has no relatives, she is also concerned as to who will take care of her 15-month-old daughter during her confinement. 17._____
 The one of the following suggestions which would be MOST helpful is that

   A. application be made to the child care division of the Department of Social Services
   B. her husband take over this responsibility
   C. a neighbor take the child into her home
   D. the child be taken to the Children's Shelter
   E. application be made to a family agency for homemaker service

Questions 18-20.

DIRECTIONS: Questions 18 through 20 are to be answered SOLELY on the basis of the facts given below.

CASE C

A woman, pregnant out of wedlock, in her 8th month of pregnancy, cones to you as the medical social worker in a city hospital, asking you to arrange for the adoption of her baby. She says she has no friends and is not interested in any plan for the baby other than adoption.

18. The one of the following agencies to which you would refer the woman described in Case C is the 18._____

   A. Spence-Chapin Adoption Service
   B. Bureau of Child Welfare of the Department of Social Services
   C. Surrogates' Court
   D. Domestic Relations Court
   E. Aid to Dependent Children Division of the Department of Social Services

19. The woman described in Case C is presently living in a furnished room and cannot pay the coming week's rent. She is Catholic and is willing to enter a shelter for unmarried mothers. 19._____
 The one of the following shelters to which you would seek admission for her is

   A. The Wm. Booth Memorial Home and Hospital
   B. Inwood House
   C. The Heartsease Home for Women and Babies
   D. St. Faith's House
   E. The Guild of the Infant Saviour

20. When the baby is ready for adoption, the one of the following courts which would have jurisdiction over the adoption proceedings is the _____ Court. 20._____

   A. Criminal
   B. Surrogates'
   C. Family Division of Domestic Relations
   D. County
   E. Children's Court of Domestic Relations

KEY (CORRECT ANSWERS)

1. C
2. A
3. A
4. B
5. D

6. B
7. E
8. A
9. C
10. D

11. B
12. D
13. A
14. E
15. B

16. B
17. A
18. B
19. E
20. B

EXAMINATION SECTION
TEST 1

DIRECTIONS: Each question or incomplete statement is followed by several suggested answers or completions. Select the one that BEST answers the question or completes the statement. *PRINT THE LETTER OF THE CORRECT ANSWER IN THE SPACE AT THE RIGHT.*

1. A medical social worker can give service to an incurably ill patient MOST effectively by

    A. urging him to sleep and rest a great deal to conserve his strength
    B. helping him to gain what satisfaction he can within the limits imposed by his illness
    C. instructing his family to give him everything he asks for
    D. limiting her visits to him so she will not tire him

2. A SOUND motive for entering the field of social work is a desire to

    A. satisfy a personal need for giving
    B. be in a position to dispense charity
    C. accumulate information concerning the behavior of maladjusted people
    D. help people whose lives are unhappy or without satisfaction

3. The one of the following which is of MOST value to a social case worker in carrying out her functions in any field of social work is a(n)

    A. full knowledge of community resources
    B. totally objective viewpoint toward hostile behavior
    C. awareness of the purposeful use of relationships
    D. mature personality free from conflicts

4. The social case worker, in giving help to a client, should use PRIMARILY

    A. the community facilities available to meet needs
    B. the resources of the patient and his immediate environment
    C. the agency policies to determine her focus
    D. psychiatric concepts of human behavior

5. A case worker who is new to the field of social work will MOST probably focus her efforts PRIMARILY on

    A. the problem as presented by the client
    B. the client in relation to his problem
    C. developing self-awareness in handling clients
    D. the emotional needs of the client

6. A social worker who cannot adhere to agency policies is MOST likely to be a person who

    A. cannot relate to people
    B. has problems centered around questions of authority
    C. has deep feelings of guilt
    D. has many domestic problems

7. The one of the following cases which a beginning social case worker would probably find the LEAST difficult to handle is one involving a(n)

   A. juvenile delinquent
   B. enuretic child
   C. normal child in need of convalescent care
   D. stuttering child

8. A social worker can BEST begin to help a couple with a marital problem by FIRST

   A. referring them to a psychiatrist
   B. referring them to the family physician for guidance
   C. suggesting that they go to court with their problem
   D. helping them to clarify for themselves the nature of their problem

9. The social case worker often finds that legally responsible relatives of her clients are hostile when expected to contribute towards support or payment of medical expenses of the client.
   The one of the following which would be the MOST desirable way of dealing with such hostility is for the social worker to

   A. look into her own background to understand why these relatives are so resistant
   B. tell the relatives that this is a legal responsibility which cannot be evaded
   C. suggest that the relatives contact their legislators toward changing this requirement
   D. acknowledge the hardships involved for relatives and give understanding and treatment of the problem involved

10. A medical social work consultant from the Crippled Children's Bureau, in helping to set up a program of convalescent care for long-term orthopedically crippled patients, should prefer foster home care to institutional care PRIMARILY because

    A. a greater degree of emotional security would thereby be provided
    B. the children could then attend public school with normal children
    C. medical care of the children would then be better
    D. the families could then visit the children more frequently

11. The one of the following statements in regard to the emotional needs and attitudes of children which is MOST accurate is that

    A. it is not possible for a working mother to meet the emotional needs of her child
    B. parents who receive public assistance cannot meet the child's need for security
    C. a child who is emotionally secure does not have feelings of aggression
    D. parental support and acceptance are important to develop a feeling of belonging in the child

12. Persistent feeding problems with nursery or school-age children are MOST probably caused by

    A. hostility toward the mother
    B. the physical make-up of the child
    C. impoverished home conditions
    D. basic personality maladjustments

13. Local health departments and crippled children's agencies are assuming more and more responsibility for the teaching of various professional groups. Medical social workers are participating actively in programs of educational institutions and in-service training.
    The CHIEF objective of such teaching by a medical social worker is to

    A. supplement the knowledge of other professional groups so that they may perform minor case work services for the patient group
    B. teach social work concepts and demonstrate the need for more extensive medical social work
    C. encourage each professional group to realize fully the need of understanding every individual
    D. bring to other professions an approach to medical social work techniques which can be integrated into their own practice

14. The provision of medical services by the Department of Social Services for its recipients is presently and has been in the past

    A. focused on rehabilitation through employment
    B. all-inclusive to meet the needs of the clients
    C. supplementary to other community health services
    D. focused primarily on the medical needs of adults

15. Assume that a child who is a ward of the Foundling Hospital and who has been in a foster home placement through that agency is admitted to a city hospital with acute appendicitis.
    The required consent for an operation MUST be obtained from the

    A. hospital superintendent   B. foster parent
    C. Foundling Hospital   D. next of kin

16. The one of the following which is the MOST important point for a medical social worker to stress in the initial orientation of a group of new case workers to the use of agency case records is the

    A. statistical use of the records
    B. confidentiality of the material
    C. value of records in court
    D. type of recording used

17. When a medical social worker in a hospital is requested to assist with the teaching of medical students, it is a CARDINAL principle that the meetings must

   A. be attended by either the supervisor or the director of the social service division
   B. be held at the hospital to give meaning to the students
   C. be sponsored by the clinical teacher of the students
   D. have a patient present for demonstration purposes

17.____

18. An employee in a social agency who is charged with administrative functions should

   A. carry personal liability insurance
   B. make his opinions subordinate to those of his staff members
   C. be willing to delegate authority
   D. make decisions regarding all matters of policy without consulting his staff members

18.____

19. In interpreting agency function and administrative structure to a group of case workers, it is important to point out that policies are set up PRIMARILY to

   A. define the duties of each worker
   B. limit the amount of expenditures
   C. obtain state or federal reimbursement
   D. provide help for client and worker

19.____

20. Consultation in social work is MOST effective when the consultee

   A. understands that such consultation is an administrative order
   B. has a set schedule for consultation conferences
   C. recognizes his need for help and requests it
   D. recognizes the superior intelligence of the consultant

20.____

Questions 21-25.

DIRECTIONS: In Questions 21 through 25, Column I lists titles of books and Column II lists authors. Select the author for each book listed in Column I and write the letter which precedes the author in the blank space at the right, which corresponds to the number of the question.

COLUMN I
21. SUPERVISION IN SOCIAL CASE WORK
22. SOCIAL WELFARE AND PROFESSIONAL EDUCATION
23. SHADOW ON THE LAND; SYPHILIS
24. THE MEANING OF DISEASE
25. SOCIAL ASPECTS OF ILLNESS

COLUMN II
A. Edith Abbott
B. Carol Cooley
C. Thomas Parran
D. G. Canby Robinson
E. Virginia P. Robinson
F. Frances Upham
G. William A. White

21.____
22.____
23.____
24.____
25.____

KEY (CORRECT ANSWERS)

1. B
2. D
3. C
4. B
5. A

6. B
7. C
8. D
9. D
10. A

11. D
12. D
13. D
14. C
15. C

16. B
17. C
18. C
19. D
20. C

21. E
22. A
23. C
24. G
25. B

TEST 2

DIRECTIONS: Each question or incomplete statement is followed by several suggested answers or completions. Select the one that BEST answers the question or completes the statement. *PRINT THE LETTER OF THE CORRECT ANSWER IN THE SPACE AT THE RIGHT.*

1. The federal government accepts a responsibility for promoting and stimulating a comprehensive health program for all our people.
   The CHIEF reason for the assumption of this responsibility is that

   A. the health of our people is probably our most important national resource
   B. in some of the states the morbidity and mortality rates are extremely high
   C. greater medical needs are emerging as the nation is getting to be *a nation of elders*
   D. the medical profession has been unable to cover the needs of the major portion of the population

1.___

2. The medical profession was at first opposed to state legislation calling for mandatory reporting by doctors of certain contagious and communicable diseases to local health departments.
   Their resistance was based PRIMARILY on the fact that they believed that

   A. this law would cause them to lose their patients
   B. the individual was more important than society
   C. this law was a violation of medical ethics
   D. this law would lead to socialized medicine

2.___

3. The state governments in the United States have traditionally assumed responsibility for caring for

   A. merchant seamen
   B. the mentally ill
   C. patients with contagious diseases
   D. victims of industrial accidents

3.___

4. The one of the following organizations which is supported from public funds is the

   A. National Institution of Health
   B. American Public Welfare Association
   C. American Public Health Association
   D. National Council on Family Relations

4.___

5. Prior to 1935, the federal government assumed medical responsibility CHIEFLY for

   A. widows and orphans B. federal employees
   C. tuberculous patients D. military personnel

5.___

6. The one of the following programs of the Social Security Act which is DIRECTLY administered by the federal government through the Social Security Administration is

   A. old age and survivors' insurance
   B. aid to the disabled
   C. aid to crippled children
   D. old age assistance

6.___

7. The Social Security Act authorizes funds to be allotted by the Children's Bureau to the states so that needed services can be made readily available to all crippled children in the state.
   In actual practice,

   A. the eligibility of a child for care is determined only on basis of medical needs
   B. states determine eligibility for service on basis of economic as well as medical needs
   C. all patients with childhood crippling conditions are accepted for care
   D. the act restricts the types of crippling conditions for which services will be available

7._____

8. The one of the following which would cause an employee to be INELIGIBLE for state unemployment insurance benefits is

   A. possession of a private unemployment insurance policy
   B. loss of job because of termination of business by employer
   C. dismissal because of seasonal layoffs
   D. dismissal because of misconduct

8._____

9. Old age and survivors' insurance and workmen's compensation are similar in that they both

   A. require a *means* test to determine eligibility for benefits
   B. are concerned with benefit rights based on past employment
   C. operate under state administration with federal guidance
   D. require court action for determination of benefits

9._____

10. In the city, shelter care for children is provided by private agencies as well as the Children's Center. The private agencies are licensed by the

    A. Department of Health
    B. Department of Welfare
    C. Department of Hospitals
    D. State Department of Social Services

10._____

11. The licensing of nursing homes in the city is the responsibility of the

    A. Department of Health
    B. Department of Hospitals
    C. Department of Social Services
    D. State Department of Social Welfare

11._____

12. A public welfare agency differs from a private welfare agency in that the former functions within

    A. administrative rules
    C. a framework of law
    B. budgetary requirements
    D. a wider geographical unit

12._____

13. Legal incorporation of a private social agency is IMPORTANT because

    A. members of the staff will then avoid personal responsibility for acts of the agency
    B. it results in greater efficiency in running the agency
    C. the agency can then solicit funds without restrictions
    D. no other agency can then be set up to carry out the same functions

14. The one of the following agencies which will cover the cost of nursing home visits to a relief recipient who is on the home care program of a city hospital is the

    A. Department of Hospitals
    B. Department of Social Services
    C. Nursing Sisters of the Sick Poor
    D. Visiting Nurse Service

15. If a child of 15 years is stricken with poliomyelitis and needs braces for which his family cannot pay, the braces can be obtained through the

    A. State Division of Vocational Rehabilitation
    B. Department of Social Services
    C. Department of Hospitals
    D. Department of Health

16. The one of the following statements which is MOST accurate in regard to the employability clinics of the Department of Social Services which are located in city hospitals is that

    A. the hospital is partially reimbursed for services rendered
    B. the Department of Social Services is able to use the facilities of the hospitals without any payment
    C. only treatment of minor ailments is available in these clinics
    D. laboratory services for the clinics are supplied by the Department of Health

17. The state will reimburse the city for the cost of hospitalization of a person receiving aid to the blind to the extent of _____ percent of the total cost.

    A. 30　　　　　B. 50　　　　　C. 80　　　　　D. 100

18. The one of the following services which is FALSE is that

    A. the Department of Social Services maintains a panel of full-time salaried physicians who devote their services to treatment of the recipients
    B. an adult, with his or her consent, may be legally adopted by another adult
    C. any client of the Department of Social Services requiring examination to determine the degree of blindness may be examined at a Department of Social Services eye clinic
    D. no minor should be treated in a hospital or clinic without written consent of a parent or guardian

4 (#2)

19. The one of the following statements which is NOT true is that the Department of Social Services

    A. does not reimburse the Department of Hospitals for out-patient service given to its clients
    B. provides drugs for its clients who receive care in an out-patient clinic of a city hospital
    C. may provide appliances for a client attending an out-patient clinic of a city hospital
    D. will pay for a client's transportation to the outpatient clinic of a voluntary hospital

19._____

20. The one of the following statements in regard to the use of statistics in social work which is MOST valid is that

    A. statistics are non-essential to budget presentation
    B. statistics speak for themselves and need no interpretation
    C. uniformity of statistical controls is unimportant
    D. statistics are essential in planning the agency program

20._____

21. The one of the following which is the LEAST accurate statement in regard to the use of statistical controls in public welfare administration is that statistics

    A. furnish conclusive evidence as to the quality of the worker's performance
    B. are required by law
    C. are an indication of the employee's use of his time
    D. can serve as a supervisory tool for evaluation of work

21._____

22. The one of the following which is set up to further the control of alcoholism is

    A. Men's Shelter   B. William Hodson Center
    C. Camp LaGuardia   D. Bridge House

22._____

23. In the city, the administrative authority for carrying out the public program for physically handicapped children rests with the _____ Department of _____.

    A. city; Health   B. city; Social Services
    C. city; Hospitals   D. state; Social Services

23._____

24. Teaching case workers how to use community resources can BEST be done by

    A. group meetings
    B. planning field trips to several agencies
    C. relating the teaching to their own cases
    D. bringing speakers to the agency staff meetings

24._____

25. If a child of 17 whose family is receiving aid to dependent children needs orthodontia, this service will be provided by the Department of

    A. Education   B. Hospitals
    C. Social Services   D. Health

25._____

KEY (CORRECT ANSWERS)

1. A
2. C
3. B
4. A
5. D

6. A
7. B
8. D
9. B
10. A

11. B
12. C
13. A
14. A
15. D

16. B
17. B
18. A
19. B
20. D

21. A
22. D
23. A
24. C
25. D

———

TEST 3

DIRECTIONS: Each question or incomplete statement is followed by several suggested answers or completions. Select the one that BEST answers the question or completes the statement. *PRINT THE LETTER OF THE CORRECT ANSWER IN THE SPACE AT THE RIGHT.*

1. Assume that you are a medical social work consultant in the Department of Social Services, and a social investigator consults you about a client who refuses needed hospitalization. The investigator feels that the client should be pressured into accepting hospital care.
   The one of the following points which you should emphasize to the investigator is

   A. the desirability of getting relatives to sway the client towards accepting hospital care
   B. agency rules against the use of pressure
   C. the client's right of self-determination
   D. legal provisions against forcing the client to accept hospital care

2. The major part of the costs of medical care for persons receiving public assistance in the city is represented by

   A. hospital costs
   B. physicians' visits
   C. nurses' visits
   D. surgical appliances

3. The Public Health Law of the state was amended to change the provisions relating to charges and reimbursement for hospital care and treatment of persons with tuberculosis. The one of the following which is MOST accurate in regard to this amendment is that

   A. the state will reimburse each locality 100% for state charges in local tuberculosis hospitals
   B. the 50% state aid formula is changed to a maximum of $5 per patient day
   C. each locality is now responsible for the total cost of the care of its own residents in tuberculosis hospitals
   D. the state will assume full responsibility for the treatment and hospitalization of all diagnosed tuberculosis patients within the state

4. The services of a panel physician may not be authorized for clients of the Department of Social Services known to be suffering from

   A. an acute upper respiratory infection
   B. any contagious disease
   C. a chronic disease
   D. an acute form of venereal disease

5. In order to function most effectively as a medical social work consultant in the Department of Social Services, it would be important for the consultant to

   A. plan weekly conferences with the individual investigators around medical problems in their cases
   B. meet regularly on a scheduled basis with the unit supervisors to discuss cases with medical aspects
   C. review all the new cases each month for medical problems
   D. interview those clients who refuse to accept recommended medical care

6. In regard to the placement of clients of the Department of Social Services in nursing homes, the one of the following statements which is NOT true is that

   A. authorization by the medical director for nursing home care must be reviewed every three months
   B. assistance may be granted to residents of only those nursing homes which are approved by the Department of Social Services
   C. placement and residence in a nursing home must have the client's full consent and cooperation
   D. a plan for nursing home care requires the approval of the unit supervisor and the medical social work consultant

7. The medical care program in the Children's Center of the Department of Social Services is the direct responsibility of the Bureau of

   A. Child Welfare
   B. Social Services
   C. Institutional Administration
   D. Welfare Administration

Questions 8-11.

DIRECTIONS: Questions 8 through 11 are to be answered on the basis of the facts given in the case described below.

CASE I

Assume that you are a medical social work consultant in the Department of Social Services and a unit supervisor asks your assistance in the following case which is being carried by one of her investigators.

A young unmarried expectant mother from another city requests help with planning for herself and her baby. Except for one visit to a doctor to determine whether or not she was pregnant, she has had no prenatal care. She is without funds and has been evicted from her furnished room because of non-payment of rent. She is hesitant about giving information about herself because she does not wish her parents to know of her pregnancy. She has written to the father of her baby, who is a sergeant in the army, informing him of her pregnancy but has received no answer from him. She speaks vaguely of boarding the baby until she gets on her feet financially.

8. The one of the following which should be the social investigator's FIRST step in helping this girl is to

   A. offer her concrete help with her immediate problems, such as finding a place to live and planning for herself and her baby
   B. urge her to tell her parents so that they might help her
   C. discuss with her the advantages and disadvantages of boarding the baby or placing it for adoption
   D. offer to contact the baby's father through Red Cross

9. The one of the following agencies which would be LEAST likely to offer a helpful service to the client in this situation is the

   A. American Red Cross
   B. Department of Welfare
   C. St. Giles' Home
   D. Foundling Hospital

10. If this girl continues to be undecided about plans for her baby, the one of the following ways in which the social investigator could BEST help her is by

   A. suggesting that she get in touch with her parents so that she might have the benefit of their advice and counsel
   B. encouraging her to evaluate all possible plans and their advantages and disadvantages for the baby and for herself
   C. supporting her inclination to keep the baby and offering to help her find a foster home
   D. suggesting that she wait until she sees the baby before she considers plans

11. The one of the following ways in which the investigator could BEST help this girl to use this experience to make a more satisfactory adjustment to life in the future is by

   A. recognizing that she is lonely and referring her to recreational resources
   B. pointing out that unmarried mothers are neurotic and referring her to a psychiatrist
   C. helping her to use the interviews with the investigator to gain some self-understanding
   D. suggesting that the patient go home after the baby is born, since she appears to be unable to make a good adjustment away from her family and friends

Questions 12-20.

DIRECTIONS: Questions 12 through 20 are to be answered on the basis of the facts given in the case described below.

CASE II

Assume that in your capacity as a medical social work consultant in the Department of Social Services, the following situation is brought to your attention by a social investigator.

Mrs. G., a thirty-five year old Catholic woman, mother of three children and now pregnant, has been deserted by her husband and applies to the Department of Social Services for financial assistance. She says she does not know where her husband is. He had supported the family by working as a longshoreman until three months ago when he was discovered to have active tuberculosis. At that time, sanatorium care was recommended but he refused to go, and soon after he deserted his family.

Mrs. G. says her only living relatives are her step-mother, who lives with her, and two married step-brothers, living in the city, who have been helping her since Mr. G. deserted, but who now feel she should get help from the Department of Social Services. Mr. G.'s only relative is his mother, living in the city.

12. In abandoning his wife while she is pregnant, Mr. G. was LEGALLY guilty of

   A. a misdemeanor   B. a felony
   C. vagrancy   D. a fraud

13. The one of the following agencies which should be contacted FIRST in attempting to locate Mr. G. is the

   A. National Desertion Bureau
   B. Federal Bureau of Investigation
   C. Department of Social Services
   D. Police Department

14. If the Department of Social Services should be notified that Mr. G. is working in the city and able, but unwilling, to contribute to his family's support, the court where the department would start action is the____ Court.

    A. Family Division of the Domestic Relations
    B. Children's Division of the Domestic Relations
    C. Criminal
    D. Supreme

15. If it is proved in this case that neither the father nor the mother is able to support the children, the LEGAL responsibility for the support of the children falls upon

    A. Mr. G.'s mother
    B. the Department of Social Services
    C. Mrs. G.'s step-mother
    D. Mrs. G.'s step-brothers

16. On the basis of Mrs. G.'s statement that her husband had active tuberculosis prior to his desertion, the social investigator on the case believes that each family member should be examined. The one of the following which would give DEFINITE evidence of active pulmonary tuberculosis in any of the family members is

    A. BCG vaccine   B. a Mantoux test
    C. a patch test   D. Roentgen study

17. The one of the following agencies to which you would refer the family for examination for tuberculosis is the

    A. nearest voluntary clinic
    B. State Tuberculosis and Health Association
    C. nearest city hospital
    D. Department of Health

18. If one of the children were found to have active pulmonary tuberculosis, the one of the following hospitals which would admit the child is _____ Hospital.

    A. St. Charles   B. Knickerbocker
    C. Seaview   D. Willowbrook

19. Mrs. G. shows concern about the care of her children during the period of her confinement. She states that if she goes to a hospital for delivery of her child, her step-mother would not be physically capable of giving them adequate care.
    In this situation, the one of the following plans which would be MOST adequate is to

    A. arrange home delivery
    B. plan for homemaker service
    C. place the children
    D. prove the step-mother's ability to care for the children

20. If Mrs. G. decides to go to a voluntary hospital clinic for prenatal care prior to delivery, the Department of Social Services will pay for

    A. medicines   B. laboratory fees
    C. x-ray examination   D. clinic fees

Questions 21-25.

DIRECTIONS: In Questions 21 through 25, Column I lists important happenings in the field of social welfare, and Column II lists dates. For each event listed in Column I, select its date from Column II, and write the letter which precedes the date in the space at the right corresponding to the number of the question.

	COLUMN I	COLUMN II	
21.	Enactment of the New York State Workmen's Compensation Law	A. 1875 B. 1910	21.____
22.	Enactment of the New York State Public Welfare Law	C. 1912 D. 1929	22.____
23.	Passage of the Social Security Act	E. 1931 F. 1933	23.____
24.	Establishment of the U.S. Children's Bureau	G. 1935	24.____
25.	Passage of the Federal Emergency Relief Act		25.____

KEY (CORRECT ANSWERS)

1.	C		11.	C
2.	A		12.	B
3.	B		13.	D
4.	D		14.	A
5.	B		15.	A
6.	A		16.	D
7.	A		17.	D
8.	A		18.	C
9.	C		19.	B
10.	B		20.	A

21. B
22. D
23. G
24. C
25. F

EXAMINATION SECTION
TEST 1

DIRECTIONS: Each question or incomplete statement is followed by several suggested answers or completions. Select the one that *BEST* answers the question or completes the statement. *PRINT THE LETTER OF THE CORRECT ANSWER IN THE SPACE AT THE RIGHT.*

1. Generally, the *MAIN* reason for using the questioning technique in a case work interview is to
    A. reveal discrepancies in information given by the client
    B. reinforce your own ideas about the case
    C. obtain necessary factual information about the client
    D. bring out the hidden motives of the client

    1.____

2. According to a basic case work principle, a worker should "accept" the client, regardless of the client's feelings, attitudes and behavior. This concept of "acceptance" means, most nearly, that the worker
    A. agrees with what the client says, does, and feels
    B. demonstrates his respect for the client as a human being
    C. has no strong opinions about the client's values
    D. thinks the way the client thinks

    2.____

3. Before visiting a new client, it is desirable for you to be prepared in advance, when possible.
    Which one of the following should generally NOT be included in these advance preparations?
    A. *Learning* as much as possible about the client from the medical chart
    B. *Trying* to put yourself in the client's place
    C. *Recognizing* your own prejudices and stereotypes
    D. *Deciding* on a solution to the client's problems

    3.____

4. After introducing yourself to a new patient, which one of the following questions generally would be the *MOST* appropriate for you to ask?
    A. "Do you expect any visitors today?"
    B. "Who is your attending physician?"
    C. "How can I be of help to you?"
    D. "Do you have hospitalization insurance?"

    4.____

5. In the middle of an interview, a patient makes a statement which seems unclear. Of the following, the *BEST* way to deal with this situation would be for the worker to
    A. ask the patient to rephrase her statement
    B. rephrase the statement, and ask the patient if that is what she meant
    C. inform the patient that she is not making herself clear
    D. let the patient finish and then try to tie the story together

    5.____

6. Assume that, at the conclusion of an interview with a client, you have reviewed problems that have been resolved. Generally, the MOST appropriate of the following closing actions for you to take would be to

    A. remind the patient to be on time for the next appointment
    B. go over specific actions that you and the client will take before the next visit
    C. remind the client to take tranquilizers when feeling upset
    D. ask the client to think of new problems to discuss during the next visit

7. Which one of the following would be a MAJOR responsibility of a worker assigned to the surgery ward?

    A. *Instructing* the nurse about changes in medication for patients
    B. *Advising* relatives of the best time to visit patients
    C. *Detecting* anxiety of patients due to their medical illness
    D. *Recording* the number of visitors received by patients

8. Assume that you have been assigned the case of an eight-year-old child whose parents were both seriously injured in an automobile accident. You realize that this child will have severe problems in the months ahead.
    During the *first* interview, of the following, the BEST way to assist the child would be to

    A. convince the child of his ability to be brave and grown-up
    B. play a competitive game with the child and let him win
    C. help the child express his fears and reassure him in accordance with reality
    D. tell the child that his problems are not so great as they may seem

9. Assume that one of your clients has many medical and social problems and needs a good deal of supportive case work help.
    Which one of the following approaches would generally be MOST appropriate for you to use in order to help this client cope with these problems?

    A. *Try* to make the client feel that his problems and situation are unique
    B. *Encourage* the client to be realistic about his situation and assure him that you understand and will do everything possible to help him cope
    C. *Emphasize* to the client those areas you feel you can work on and those which you can do nothing about
    D. *Urge* the client to refrain from taking action on serious matters without asking for your help first

10. Assume that, when you discuss with one of your elderly clients the advisability of applying to the department of socital services for financial assistance, the client becomes extremely upset about the prospect of having to be interviewed by "another stranger."
    Of the following, the BEST way to handle this situation would be to

    A. explain that applying for financial assistance is something the client must do by herself and for herself
    B. offer to accompany the client to social services if necessary, and work with the client toward greater future independence
    C. withdraw your suggestion, since the client's emotional health is your primary consideration
    D. suggest that the client take a personal friend to the interview to help with difficult questions, if necessary

11. Assume that a newspaper reporter calls and questions you regarding the long wait for treatment in the Emergency Room. Of the following, your MOST appropriate response would be to

    A. advise the reporter that the long wait is caused by an enormous increase in emergency cases
    B. refer the reporter to the director of social work
    C. tell the reporter that your hospital's emergency room is one of the most efficient in the city
    D. refer the reporter to the hospital employee responsible for public relations

12. When a worker interviews a patient whose problem seems to be typical of that of many other patients she has seen, of the following, it would be MOST appropriate to

    A. *attempt* to learn more about the individual circumstances of this patient's situation
    B. *handle* this case the same way as the others were handled
    C. *ask* another worker how she generally handles this type of problem
    D. *reassure* the patient by telling him that many other patients have similar problems

13. A patient without friends or relatives is being discharged from the hospital. He complains to you that his shoes are missing.
    Of the following, your MOST appropriate response would be to

    A. advise the patient that this is not a professional concern of yours and suggest that he speak to the ward nurse
    B. advise the patient that he will have to buy a pair of shoes from a nearby shoe store
    C. obtain a pair of shoes for the patient in the hospital clothing room
    D. tell the patient that he probably was not wearing shoes at the time he was admitted

14. The parents of a hospitalized child complain to you that their child is not getting proper nursing care. You have ample opportunity to observe what is happening on the pediatric ward and know that the nurses are extremely conscientious in caring for the children. Your *initial* interpretation of this complaint should be that, probably, the parents

    A. are projecting their anxiety about the child's health by criticizing the nurses
    B. are chronic complainers and must be treated accordingly
    C. may actually want to transfer the child to a more conveniently located hospital
    D. are trying to get special treatment for their child from the nurses

15. You are interviewing an unmarried, attractive young female patient who was in an automobile accident and will not be able to walk again. She says to you: "I'll never find a husband now that I'm crippled."
    In order to help her express her feelings freely, of the following, your MOST appropriate response would be:

    A. "You feel that no one will marry you because you can't walk."
    B. "Don't be silly. You have your whole life ahead of you."
    C. "That's not necessarily true. You're young and pretty and smart."
    D. "That may be true, but at least you're alive."

16. Assume that you are in your office completing some paperwork. A man enters and introduces himself as a close friend of one of your patients in the terminal cancer ward. He then asks if he can speak with you, and sits down in the chair next to your desk.
    Of the following, it would be MOST appropriate for you to say FIRST:

    A. "You probably want to know how your friend is coping with his condition."
    B. "You realize, of course, that your friend is dying of cancer."
    C. "What would you like to see me about?"
    D. "What problem would you like to discuss?"

17. During an interview with a new patient your mind wanders momentarily, and you have missed some details in the patient's story.
    Which one of the following would be most appropriate to say FIRST, before the patient continues?

    A. "And then what happened?" – so that the patient will think that you were paying attention all along.
    B. "Could you rephrase that?" – so that the patient will restate the details without being aware of your inattentiveness.
    C. "I'm sorry, I didn't get that, could you repeat that part?" – so that the patient will perceive you as an honest person.
    D. "Please continue". – so that the patient will not have to repeat something that was probably unimportant anyway.

18. Assume that one of your clients is telling you about her family situation. All of a sudden, she says: "Two of my kids go to school, and the third, who is seventeen, ..."
    Then she stops speaking.
    In this situation, of the following, it would be most appropriate for you to FIRST

    A. *state:* "works?"
    B. *state:* "quit school?"
    C. *ask:* "What about the third child?"
    D. *remain silent* for a few seconds

19. You have just started to interview a new client. He begins by telling you that he has been unemployed for the past three years and is receiving almost as much from welfare as he did when he was working. He continues talking along these lines, and then asks you why anybody would want to work when they can be on the dole and maintain almost the same standard of living.
    Of the following, your MOST appropriate response would be:

    A. "I don't personally approve of living in that manner."
    B. "It all depends on a person's values and standards."
    C. "If you are happy living like that, it's all right with me."
    D. "Let's not discuss that. Let's talk about your medical problems first."

20. During your second interview with a young woman, she asks you to drop all this professional stuff and just be friends.
Which one of the following would be your appropriate response?

    A. "If we were friends, I would probably not be so effective in helping you deal with your problem."
    B. "That's O.K. with me, but you would have to be reassigned to a different worker."
    C. "That would be impossible under the rules and regulations of our agency."
    D. "I really don't think that's appropriate, and I'm a very busy person."

20._____

KEY (CORRECT ANSWERS)

1.	C	11.	D
2.	B	12.	A
3.	D	13.	C
4.	C	14.	A
5.	A	15.	A
6.	B	16.	C
7.	C	17.	C
8.	C	18.	D
9.	B	19.	B
10.	B	20.	A

TEST 2

DIRECTIONS: Each question or incomplete statement is followed by several suggested answers or completions, Select the one that *BEST* answers the question or completes the statement. *PRINT THE LETTER OF THE CORRECT ANSWER IN THE SPACE AT THE RIGHT.*

1. You are interviewing a young man who confides, in you that he is now on probation. In order to help this patient, you decide that it would be desirable to contact his probation officer to obtain additional information.
   Of the following, the BEST way to contact the probation officer would be

   A. *after* the interview, with the patient's consent
   B. *after* the interview, without the patient's consent
   C. *after* the interview, without telling the patient
   D. *during* the interview, with the patient present

   1.____

2. You introduce yourself to a newly-hospitalized patient and offer to be of assistance if possible. The patient nods that she understands, and begins to discuss her 12-year-old daughter's truancy from school.
   Which one of the following responses would be most appropriate for you to make FIRST?

   A. *I understand your daughter's problem, but can we discuss your problems now?*
   B. *How do you feel this will affect you while you are in the hospital?*
   C. *Did your daughter fail any of her subjects because of her truancy?*
   D. *I have a very large caseload today. Perhaps we can discuss your daughter another time.*

   2.____

3. You have been interviewing a patient for almost an hour and it is time for your next appointment. As you are about to finish, the patient begins to discuss a new problem.
   In this situation, it would generally be advisable to

   A. close the interview and make another appointment with the patient to discuss this problem
   B. allow the patient to *get things off his chest* before closing the interview
   C. ask the patient why he brought this problem up at the last moment
   D. tell the patient that you cannot discuss this problem because you will be late for your next appointment

   3.____

4. Assume that you are completing a case involving a deteriorating relationship between the parents of a child who was hospitalized due to an accident caused by the child's father. Since counselling began upon admission of the child, there has been a marked improvement in the relationship between the parents and, in particular, between the child and the father. The child is about to be discharged from the hospital, and you are having an interview with the parents.
   Of the following, according to accepted casework practice, it would be MOST appropriate for you to

   A. assure the parents that, as a result of counselling, they are now *ideal* parents
   B. offer a continuation of counselling until the family's adjustment is stable
   C. review with the parents the *do's and don'ts* of being *good* parents
   D. explain to the parents how you helped them solve their problems

   4.____

5. Assume that one of your clients, an adult male out-patient who has been coming to see you weekly for four months, fails to keep two appointments. The physician informs you that one of this patient's laboratory tests is positive, indicating the urgent need for follow-up medical care. You have sent the patient a telegram, but he has not replied after a reasonable length of time.
According to accepted casework practice, of the following, the MOST advisable action for you to take would be to

   A. contact a neighbor of the patient and ask the neighbor to persuade the patient to return to the hospital
   B. inform a member of the patient's family of the positive; test result and emphasize the urgency of the situation
   C. write to the patient and explain the dangers of not returning to the hospital for treatment
   D. make an emergency visit to the patient at home and tell him about the positive test result and the importance of returning to the hospital

6. Assume that you are trying to establish the identity of an elderly woman who was brought to the Emergency Room by the police, who found her on the street, somewhat disoriented. The doctor decides to admit the woman, whose blood pressure is elevated, and who has an open ulcerated wound on her leg. She is very talkative about events long in the past, can't recall where she lives, but keeps speaking of having to *go home to give her sister breakfast*. The police have found that she has a card giving her name and an address which is three blocks from the hospital, but the telephone company has no listing for her.
Of the following, your MOST advisable action would be to

   A. ask the hospital security guards to make a visit to the address on the card and tell any relatives of the woman that she is hospitalized
   B. have a visiting nurse make a visit to the address and check on the sister's possible need for food and medical attention
   C. call the social service exchange to determine whether the woman is known to any agency and what information they may have about her and her sister
   D. make a visit to the address on the card in order to obtai more information about the woman

7. You are a worker assigned to the alcoholism clinic. One of your clients appears for an interview in an intoxicated condition. Of the following, your MOST appropriate action would be to

   A. discuss the patient's drinking problem with him in no uncertain terms
   B. make another appointment and point out to the patient that he cannot be interviewed while intoxicated
   C. threaten to close the case and discharge the patient if he does not sober up
   D. recommend psychological testing to determine why the patient persists in drinking in spite of counselling

8. As a worker in the family planning clinic, you are counselling an 18-year-old unmarried patient who is pregnant. She is in a state of conflict, because she wants an abortion, but her boyfriend is encouraging her to marry him and bear the child.
Of the following, your MOST appropriate action would be to

   A. ask the patient why she was careless after receiving guidance from the family planning clinic
   B. encourage the patient to make the decision for herself, and Be supportive of her choice
   C. stress the positive qualities of her boyfriend, who is offering to marry her
   D. determine whether the conflict may derive from the patient's religious upbringing

9. Assume that one of your cases, a woman who has given birth three days ago, is now verbally abusive to the staff, and refuses to see her infant. Of the following, your MOST appropriate course of action would be to

   A. scold the woman for her childish behavior
   B. attempt to convince the woman that once she sees the baby she will feel much better
   C. speak with the woman in an effort to understand her behavior
   D. tell the woman that she will be transferred to the psychiatric unit if she does not behave

10. Assume that you are interviewing an unmarried female patient in the Emergency Room. The doctor has just told her that she must be admitted to the hospital on an emergency basis, but she refuses to accept this recommendation because she has three small children, has no one to care for them, and does not want to leave them alone.
Of the following, the most appropriate action for you to take FIRST would be to

    A. suggest that the patient try to enlist neighbors to help look after the children
    B. ask the doctor to admit the children with their mother on an emergency basis
    C. try to locate the children's father and ask him to look after the children
    D. explain to the patient that it is possible for you to arrange for care of the children

11. Assume that you are assigned to the methadone maintenance clinic. As you are about to finish an interview, your client asks you to lend him ten dollars. Of the following, your most appropriate FIRST action would be to

    A. inform the client that it is against hospital policy for a worker to lend money to a patient
    B. lend the client the ten dollars
    C. suggest that the client borrow the money from a personal friend
    D. advise the client to apply to the department of social services for an emergency grant

12. You are interviewing a young unmarried woman who is pregnant, says that she is not sure she can care for her baby properly, and is considering requesting an abortion. Of the following, your MOST appropriate response would be:

    A. *What do you think of as proper care for your baby?*
    B. *I'm sure you will be an excellent mother.*
    C. *Do you know who the father is?*
    D. *How long have you been pregnant?*

13. You are interviewing a married patient with two young children with regard to her impending surgery. Suddenly, she asks if you are married. Of the following, the MOST appropriate response would be to tell her

    A. whether you are married, and then ask why she wants to know
    B. you are not now married, but that you are engaged to be married
    C. this is irrelevant, and continue discussing her situation
    D. you used to be married, but that you are now divorced

14. You are visiting a new patient on your assigned ward. After introducing yourself and offering to be of assistance, the patient begins to tell you a lengthy story relating to her illness. According to accepted interviewing techniques, of the following, it would be MOST appropriate for you to indicate your concern and interest by

    A. briefly commenting or asking questions, indicating that you are grasping the essential points
    B. saying nothing, so as not to interrupt the patient's train of thought
    C. interrupting frequently to clarify points you do not fully comprehend
    D. asking the patient to pause at periodic intervals so that you may proceed to ask structured questions

15. You have been counseling an adult patient on the cancer ward on a weekly basis for about a month and it is now time to decide where the patient will live after being discharged from the hospital.
    According to accepted practice, the FINAL decision on this matter should be made by

    A. you, the case worker
    B. the patient's relatives
    C. the patient, with the case worker's help
    D. the patient and the doctors

16. Assume that a patient in your caseload asks you for specific advice regarding his unhappy marital situation. In deciding whether to respond to this request, you should generally consider all of the following EXCEPT

    A. any possible underlying anxiety the patient may have
    B. the patient's ability to carry out the advice
    C. the seriousness of the patient's situation
    D. whether the client will accept or reject your advice

17. According to accepted casework practice, when interviewing a young child it is considered especially important for the worker to closely observe the child's behavior, feelings, and mood, in addition to listening to what the child says, MAINLY because such observation should

    A. provide significant diagnostic information about the child
    B. help the child feel closer to the worker
    C. enable the worker to sense the right time to console the child
    D. give the worker clues as to when to humor the child

18. You find it necessary to refer a client for psychiatric help upon discharge. The client consents to this plan, but asks you to omit from your report certain information he has told you in confidence. You feel that the psychiatrist's knowledge of this information would be of great benefit in helping your client.
    For you to go ahead and include this information in your report to the psychiatrist, without the client's consent, would be considered

    A. *good practice*, because the psychiatrist will need all available information about the client
    B. *bad practice*, because this action would be a breach of confidence
    C. *good practice*, because helping the client is the primary goal of case work
    D. *bad practice*, because the patient would probably find out eventually that this information was disclosed

18._____

19. You are interviewing a woman who has suffered a severe beating from her husband, is obviously upset, and embarrassed about having to relate the details to you.
    Of the following, the MOST appropriate way for you to handle this situation would be to

    A. insist that she tell you the whole story, including the details
    B. postpone discussion of the beating until the woman feels better
    C. tell the woman to omit the details for now, and ask her how you can be of help
    D. postpone this interview until the husband is available to present his side of the story

19._____

20. You are making discharge plans for an alert, 78-year-old retired school teacher who is recovering satisfactorily from a minor operation. One day, when you come to her room, she fails to recognize you and tells you disconnected stories about people she knew in childhood.
    Of the following, the MOST appropriate way to handle this changed situation would be to

    A. tell the patient she had better *snap out of it*
    B. advise the patient that you will return when she starts talking sense
    C. confer with the attending physician about this change in the patient's condition
    D. suggest to the physician that the discharge plan be changed to recommend admission to a State hospital

20._____

KEY (CORRECT ANSWERS)

1.	A		11.	A
2.	B		12.	A
3.	A		13.	A
4.	B		14.	A
5.	D		15.	C
6.	D		16.	D
7.	B		17.	A
8.	B		18.	B
9.	C		19.	C
10.	D		20.	C

EXAMINATION SECTION
TEST 1

DIRECTIONS: Each question or incomplete statement is followed by several suggested answers or completions. Select the one the BEST answers the question or completes the statement. *PRINT THE LETTER OF THE CORRECT ANSWER IN THE SPACE AT THE RIGHT.*

1. The primary sources of data in most assessments are

    A. completed assessment forms
    B. the client's verbal statements
    C. psychological test results
    D. collateral sources

    1.____

2. A social worker is fulfilling the role of a "mediator" when he or she

    A. calls attention to the probable social consequences to a new housing development
    B. refers a jobless person to an unemployment agency
    C. evaluates the outcome of a colleague's practice
    D. helps a frustrated wife to clarify her position to a husband

    2.____

3. In the systems model of human behavior, "division of labor" is an example of

    A. autopoiesis
    B. social control
    C. differentiation
    D. hierarchy

    3.____

4. After several weeks of behavioral intervention, a child is consistently performing the desired behavior targeted by his parents and a social worker: that is, he is going to bed at the correct time without argument or delaying tactics. Now that he's reached this stage, the social worker recommends that the parents gradually withdraw the prompts and reinforcements that induced the behavior to begin with. This is an example of

    A. extinction
    B. shaping
    C. fading
    D. modeling

    4.____

5. When working with a group, a social worker encourages decision-making by consensus. Drawbacks to the use of consensus include

    A. involvement of few available group resources
    B. alienation of the minority
    C. time- and energy-intensiveness
    D. decreased likelihood of handling future controversies

    5.____

6. The primary rationale for the use of a social history for client assessment is that

    A. past behavior is the best predictor of future behavior
    B. the best source of information about a client's situation is the client her/himself
    C. the best protection against legal liability is an exhaustive data set

    6.____

D. problems exist because of an unbalanced reaction between a client system and the environment

7. Most professional codes of ethics provide that a social worker's primary ethical duty is to

   A. respect client privacy and confidentiality
   B. challenge social injustice
   C. work in the best interest of clients
   D. avoid situations that involve ethical conflicts

8. In agency planning, which of the following visual aids will be MOST useful in helping to examine the benefits and drawbacks of different alternative choices

   A. Task planning sheet
   B. Gantt chart
   C. Decision tree
   D. PERT chart

9. Which of the following questions or statements is MOST appropriate for a practitioner in initiating an interview?

   A. "I understand you have a problem."
   B. "You came in here to see me about _____."
   C. "How can I help you today?"
   D. "I'm glad you came in to see me

10. What is the term commonly used to describe children who suffer physical, mental, or emotional injuries inflicted by caretaking adults?

    A. Developmentally disabled
    B. Victims
    C. At risk
    D. Abused or neglected

11. Typically, the questioning process in a social work interview should progress

    A. chronologically
    B. from general to specific
    C. from specific to general
    D. in a series of grouped topical units

12. Assessment is a process that is considered to be the task of the

    A. agency psychiatrist or clinician
    B. social worker
    C. client
    D. social worker and client together

13. A social worker who wants to use a small group as a resource for clients should remember the general rule that the addition of new members, especially resistant ones, should be avoided during the _____ stage of group development.

    A. differentiation
    B. intimacy

C. preaffiliation
D. power and control

14. During an assessment interview with a male high school student, it becomes clear to the practitioner that the boy's behavior problems are related in some way to his frustration at the different expectations of his teachers and his peers concerning the role of a student. The boy is experiencing

   A. inter-role conflict
   B. role ambiguity
   C. intra-role conflict
   D. role incapacity

15. When considering the use of informal resources for an intervention, the social worker should

   A. view informal resources as an inexpensive alternative to formal services
   B. whenever possible, try to "professionalize" or train informal resources to lend them authority
   C. already have some knowledge of available self-help groups in the community
   D. whenever informal resources are identified, try to steer clients toward the ones that are probably most useful

16. Probably the biggest difference between the supervisory role in social work and that of other professions is the

   A. amount of psychological support that must be provided to supervisees
   B. degree of direct involvement in the work of supervisees
   C. predominant use of "soft' criteria in performance evaluations
   D. greater difficulty in matching workers to tasks

17. A social worker is interviewing a woman in a mental hospital who appears lucid but is suspected of having some mental illness. When gathering information, the worker should

   A. explain fully the reason for the interview and ask the client to give her opinion of her mental status
   B. ask short, closed-ended assessment questions up front
   C. administer a standardized assessment that may be evaluated by a psychologist
   D. work assessment questions into the ordinary flow of the conversation

18. A social worker becomes aware of a colleague's incompetent or unethical practice. According to the NASW code, the worker's FIRST obligation is to

   A. inform all of the colleague's relevant clients of the situation
   B. approach the colleague to discuss his/her incapacitation, incompetence, etc.
   C. file a complaint with the NASW
   D. file a complaint with the appropriate licensing board

19. A "communication loop" is completed when

   A. the person to whom the message is addressed begins to respond
   B. the person who initiates the message has completed the transmission
   C. the person to whom the message is addressed receives the message
   D. the person to whom the message is addressed decodes the message

20. Because many parents believe in and utilize corporal punishment as discipline, a social worker must be able to differentiate physical abuse from ordinary spanking or corporal punishment. Which of the following is NOT a useful means of making this distinction?

    A. Parent striking the child in places that are easily injured
    B. Repeated episodes of corporal punishment
    C. Child's report that punishments are severe and painful
    D. Injury to child's body tissue

21. A social worker makes an initial in-home visit to a married couple who have willingly submitted to an intervention regarding their marital problems. During the interview the couple points out that they will be leaving the area in a few weeks, because the wife has been transferred by her employer to a new location. Probably the MOST appropriate plan for dealing with this couple would involve the _____ model of social work.

    A. person-centered
    B. cognitive-behavioral
    C. solution-focused
    D. task-centered

22. The primary purpose of evaluative research in social work is to

    A. measure a client's self-satisfaction
    B. determine whether outcomes can be attributed to an intervention
    C. express the effectiveness of interventions in material terms
    D. determine whether an outcome was achieved

23. Each of the following should be used as a guideline in child placement decisions, EXCEPT

    A. efforts to protect the child should involve as little disruption as possible
    B. use of placement to compel a parent to take some action
    C. involvement of parents and child in the placement decision
    D. maintenance of child's cultural beliefs in placement

24. Which of the following is NOT a factor involved in the decoding of a message?

    A. Relationship with interviewer
    B. Social, emotional, and cognitive barriers
    C. Ethics
    D. Context of interview

25. A practitioner wants to make the parents of an adolescent aware of the behavioral manifestations of depression. Which of the following is LEAST likely to be an indicator?

    A. Sudden tearful reactions
    B. Excessive pleasure-seeking
    C. Decline in school achievement
    D. Jokes about death or dying

26. Which of the following is LEAST likely to be an area of conflict between social workers and attorneys

A. Confidentiality
B. Recording information
C. The best interests of a client
D. The definition of "client"

27. Which of the following typically occurs in the first stage of group therapy?

    A. The members are hostile toward the leader.
    B. Cliques form within the group.
    C. The members talk through the leader and seem to ignore one another.
    D. The members interact with each other tend to ignore the leader.

28. In conducting employee evaluations, a social work supervisor should use _____ as available criteria.
    I.   pre-established objective measures such as timeliness
    II. "soft" criteria such as attitude
    III. the supervisor's own work experience
    IV. the performance of others in similar assignments

    A. I only
    B. I and II
    C. I and III
    D. I, II, III and IV

29. Which of the following is NOT a term that is interchangeable with "stepfamily"?

    A. Remarried family
    B. Blended family
    C. Reconstituted family
    D. Renested family

30. A worker refers a client to a colleague who specializes and is trained in law, even though the client requested the service from the worker. Which of the following professional values or ethics is the worker implementing?

    A. Self-determination
    B. Privacy
    C. Competence
    D. Confidentiality

31. Social work practice that is based on behavioral theory assumes that behaviors are determined by

    A. emotions
    B. consequences
    C. values
    D. internal thought processes

32. Which of the following is NOT a symptom associated with bipolar disorder?

    A. Increase in goal-oriented activity
    B. Distractibility
    C. Significant weight loss
    D. Decreased need for sleep

33. A 'helping relationship" between the social worker and client is BEST described as

   A. the goal of any initial contact between worker and client
   B. the medium offered to people in trouble through which they are presented with opportunities
   C. the means by which a worker gains the client's trust to solve problems
   D. a lifeline that is thrown to people in trouble in order to help them out of current problems

34. Communities often contain individuals who are categorized as "AFDC mothers" or "hard-core unemployed" or "AIDS patients," among others. This is a destructive application of the concept of

   A. service delivery
   B. niche
   C. differentiation
   D. diversity

35. The first step in any single-system practice evaluation is to

   A. record baseline data
   B. select suitable measures
   C. implement the intervention
   D. specify the goal

36. A social worker plans a behavioral intervention for a developmentally disabled adult who does not look people in the eye when speaking with them.
   Each of the following behavioral strategies may be useful to the intervention, EXCEPT

   A. overcorrection
   B. instruction
   C. prompting
   D. shaping

37. During several in-home visits with a family, the mother repeatedly refuses to acknowledge that her alcoholism is having an adverse effect on others in the household. The MOST appropriate next step for the social worker would be to initiate

   A. a challenge
   B. behavioral rehearsal
   C. self-talk management
   D. a behavioral contract

38. Working-class or low-income marriages are typically characterized by

   A. marriage late in life
   B. flexible divisions of labor
   C. troubled mother-child relationships
   D. emotional distance between partners

39. A researcher repeatedly measures the dependent variable throughout two baseline and two treatment phases of a study to assess whether variability in the dependent variable is due to the influence of the independent variable. She is using a(n) _____ design of measurement.

A. AB
B. ABAB
C. multiple baseline
D. Solomon four-group

40. What is the typical time-frame for crisis intervention?

    A. One to two weeks
    B. Six to eight weeks
    C. At least eight weeks
    D. Six months or more, depending on the nature of the crisis

41. Stigma, once it has become part of a culture, has certain predictable consequences. Which of the following is NOT one of these consequences?

    A. Discrimination
    B. Absorption
    C. Altered self-concept
    D. Development of subculture

42. A social worker is engaged in a one-on-one interview with a 10-year-old boy, in order to investigate allegations of a father's sexual abuse. The allegations were initially brought by the mother, now divorced from the father, and were later corroborated by the boy. The mother and father are engaged in a custody battle for the boy. The boy's account of events is extremely consistent over time, listing the same major events in sequence, but his affect is flathe relates his accounts of abuse in an oddly detached manner. The BEST action for the social worker at this point would be to

    A. terminate the interview and begin criminal proceedings against the father
    B. terminate the interview and refer the child for an immediate psychiatric consultation
    C. ask the mother to join in the interview and see if her account matches the boy's
    D. ask the boy to go into greater detail about the related events, out of sequence, and then repeat the request at a later time

43. When working with individuals or families of native American cultures, it is best to begin by

    A. gathering a social history
    B. using indirect approaches such as analogy or metaphor
    C. asking for open-ended descriptions of family roles
    D. direct questioning

44. In cases of elder abuse, the government may intervene if
    I. the older person requests it
    II. the older person is found at a hearing to be incompetent
    III. the abuse or neglect presents an unacceptable level of danger to the older person
    IV. the abuse is properly reported and recorded by a visiting social services worker

    A. I only
    B. I and II

C. I, II and III
D. I, II, III and IV

45. Which of the following is a guideline that should be observed in developing an assessment questionnaire for clients?

    A. Develop several focused questionnaires rather than a single all-purpose one.
    B. The most sensitive or probing questions should appear near the middle of the questionnaire.
    C. For complex ideas, form two-part questions.
    D. Include only open-ended questions.

46. During the assessment phase of an interview, checklists are most useful for identifying and selecting

    A. problems for intervention
    B. specific objectives
    C. available resources
    D. general goals

47. Which of the following is an advantage associated with the family life-cycle model?

    A. It highlights the special challenges of blended families.
    B. It identifies developmental tasks for families at specific stages.
    C. It is especially applicable to families in minority groups.
    D. It applies to those who do not have children.

48. Before making the decision to advocate on behalf of a client, it is important to consider several factors. Which of the following is NOT one of these?

    A. Client's consent for advocacy.
    B. Whether advocating is the most useful process that can be applied to the situation.
    C. Whether the complaint or decision involves a legitimate grievance
    D. Client's knowledge and feeling about human services.

49. Which of the following is an advantage associated with the use of genograms in client assessment?

    A. Targeting and identification of relevant social supports.
    B. Execution and interpretation require no instruction.
    C. Placement of an individual or family within a social context.
    D. A considerable shortening of the case record.

50. Activities involved in social casework typically include

    A. counseling those with a terminal illness
    B. supervising juvenile probation clients
    C. providing job training
    D. preparing court reports

51. In middle childhood, school-age children are generally concerned with

    A. "good" behavior in order to receive approval from others
    B. behaving appropriately because they fear punishment

C. the concordance of behaviors with an adopted moral code
D. conforming with group standards in order to be rewarded

52. When a social worker/client relationship is characterized by ineffectiveness, the most common reason is that

    A. resources are not available to meet the client's needs
    B. the client has not sufficiently specified his or her needs
    C. an incorrect solution has been identified by the worker
    D. the worker is attempting to keep the relationship on a pleasant level

53. A social history report includes the statement: "The subject claims to have completed high school." This should be included under the heading:

    A. Family Background and Situation
    B. Intellectual functioning
    C. Impressions and Assessment
    D. Such a statement shouldn't appear at all in a social history report.

54. According to Erickson, which of the following stages of psychosocial development occurs FIRST in the human life span?

    A. Initiative vs. guilt
    B. Trust vs. mistrust
    C. Identity vs. role confusion
    D. Autonomy vs. shame and doubt

55. The strategy of "reframing" is most useful for

    A. desensitizing clients to past trauma
    B. classifying client/family problems according to standard diagnostic categories
    C. helping clients to model their own behavior after others'
    D. revealing a client's strengths and opportunities for helping

56. In general, it is believed that interviewers who spend less than a minimum of _____ of an interview listening to the client are more active than they should be.

    A. one-fourth
    B. one-third
    C. one-half
    D. two thirds

57. In the _____ model of social work, the goal of the social worker is to enhance and restore the psychosocial functioning of persons, or to change noxious social conditions that impede the mutually beneficial interaction between person and their environment.

    A. structural-functional
    B. ecological
    C. medical
    D. strategic

58. In social work, "micro" practice usually focuses on

   A. resolving the problems of individuals, families, or small groups
   B. planning, administration, evaluation, and community organizing
   C. developmental activities in the social environment
   D. facilitating communication, mediation, and negotiation

59. _____ theory may prove most productive for the social work practitioner in understanding families of homosexuals, because it introduces unambiguous distinctions between stigma and homosexual behaviors and feelings.

   A. Structural
   B. Object relations
   C. Strategic
   D. Labeling

60. A client tells a practitioner that his main goal for intervention is to decide on a college major. To BEST help this client, the practitioner will assume the role of

   A. enabler
   B. mediator
   C. initiator
   D. educator

61. Which of the following is NOT a guideline for interacting with clients from a Latino culture?

   A. Efforts to foster independence and self-reliance may be interpreted by many Latinos as a lack of concern for others.
   B. Efforts to deal one-on-one with an adolescent client may serve to alienate the parents, especially the mother.
   C. A nonverbal gesture such as lowering the eyes is interpreted by many Latinos as a sign of respect and deference to authority.
   D. In much of Latino culture, the locus of control for problems tends to be much more external than internal.

62. The broadest, most general type of plan used in social work administration is the

   A. plan for meeting objectives
   B. statement of goals
   C. statement of mission
   D. guiding policies

63. In composing a social network grid with a client, which of the following steps is typically performed FIRST?

   A. Dividing acquaintances according to direction of help
   B. Dividing acquaintances according to duration of acquaintance
   C. Identifying people who can help the client in concrete ways
   D. Identifying areas of life in which people impact the client

64. An administrator notices, in several trips through the agency grounds, that a handful of the organization's support staff are often engaged in socializing or other nonproductive activities. The groups are always small and never made up of the same people, and nearly all members of the support staff have received satisfactory evaluations from their supervisor. The socializing does not occur around clients or visiting professionals. Over the past several years, the agency's efficiency record has remained about the same. The agency would probably be BEST served by the view that

    A. rigid controls should be implemented to reduce this behavior
    B. a memorandum should be circulated citing this behavior as a poor example
    C. the behavior may help to relieve boredom and should be ignored
    D. the supervisor should add an item or two to the evaluation that will address this behavior

65. Each of the following is a stage of the dying process described by Kübler-Ross, EXCEPT

    A. acknowledgement
    B. depression
    C. anger
    D. acceptance

66. For a prison inmate, "notice of rights" means the inmate
    I. receives advance notice of what conduct will result in discipline or punishment
    II. receives written notice of any charges against him
    III. is entitled to organize a group meeting for political purposes

    A. I and II
    B. I and III
    C. II and III
    D. I, II and III

67. Which of the following values is NOT generally indigenous to families of Asian heritage?

    A. Inconspicuousness
    B. Perfectionism
    C. Fatalism
    D. Shame as a behavioral influence

68. Most professionals recommend that in order to accurately evaluate the effect of an intervention, baseline data should be collected for no fewer than _____ data points.

    A. 2
    B. 3
    C. 4
    D. 5

69. During an assessment interview, a social worker and a client try to clarify and analyze the client's sense of self. If the worker wants to discover something about the client's self-acceptance, which of the following questions is MOST appropriate?

    A. To what extent do you worry about illness and physical incapacity?
    B. Is what you expect to happen mostly good or mostly bad?

C. Do you enjoy the times when you are alone?
D. Where do your other family members live?

70. Which of the following cognitive traits explains the mistaken belief held by many adolescents that they are invincible or protected from harmful consequences of their behavior?

    A. The personal fable
    B. Object delusion
    C. Egocentrism
    D. Pseudohypocrisy

71. An 18-year-old woman comes to see a social worker at a crisis center one day after being raped on a date. In the interview with this client, the social worker should FIRST:

    A. emphasize medical and legal procedures
    B. obtain factual information about the rape
    C. listen to the client and support her emotionally
    D. help the client establish contact with significant others

72. During a client assessment, each of the following should be considered a useful question, EXCEPT

    A. Can you tell me about times when you've successfully handled a problem like this in the past?
    B. When family members complain about your behavior, what to they say?
    C. How have you managed to cope up to this point?
    D. What do your friends and family seem to like most about you?

73. Norms are MOST accurately described as

    A. attitudes toward life events and processes
    B. assumptions about the world
    C. expectations of the self and others
    D. ideas about what is proper and desirable behavior

74. Generally, when a homeless person or group is removed from a condemned or abandoned property under the law, the most significant legal question to arise is whether

    A. the last owner of the property can be located for consent
    B. the property is being "rehabilitated" by the occupants
    C. the state recognizes a "right to shelter"
    D. the property has really been abandoned

75. A social worker introduces herself to a family household in which an elderly man lives. The man has been reported by neighbors on several occasions for making threats of violence to a number of adolescents in the neighborhood. The worker recognizes that she is uninvited, and the BEST way for her to describe the purpose of her relationship to the family would be as

A. helping the man to modify his behavior so that no further institutional involvement will be necessary
B. helping the man to avoid the aggravating stimulus of contact with neighborhood teens
C. protecting the neighborhood from the elderly man's threats
D. arranging for the man to get counseling in order to understand and change his behavior

---

KEY (CORRECT ANSWERS)

1. B	16. A	31. B	46. D	61. D
2. D	17. D	32. C	47. B	62. C
3. C	18. B	33. B	48. D	63. D
4. C	19. A	34. B	49. D	64. C
5. C	20. C	35. D	50. A	65. A
6. A	21. C	36. A	51. A	66. A
7. C	22. B	37. A	52. D	67. B
8. C	23. B	38. D	53. D	68. B
9. B	24. C	39. B	54. B	69. C
10. B	25. B	40. B	55. D	70. A
11. B	26. C	41. B	56. D	71. C
12. D	27. C	42. D	57. B	72. B
13. D	28. B	43. B	58. A	73. D
14. C	29. D	44. B	59. D	74. B
15. C	30. C	45. A	60. A	75. A

TEST 2

DIRECTIONS: Each question or incomplete statement is followed by several suggested answers or completions. Select the one that BEST answers the question or completes the statement. *PRINT THE LETTER OF THE CORRECT ANSWER IN THE SPACE AT THE RIGHT.*

1. A 24-year-old mother of four, recently widowed, tells a practitioner: "I feel like my whole life has just fallen apart. I don't think I can take care of my family on my own. My husband always made all the decisions and earned the money to support us. I haven't slept well since he died and I've started drinking more often. My parents try to help me but it's not enough."
The practitioner responds by saying: "So you're afraid about your ability to shoulder all the family responsibilities now." This response is an example of a(n)

   A. reflection
   B. clarification
   C. paraphrase
   D. summarization

2. At the beginning of an intake interview, a social worker's tasks are to
   I. gather data and conduct an assessment
   II. establish a positive relationship with the interviewee
   III. obtain brief details that will indicate whether the situation for which the client wants help is among the problems for which the worker offers help
   IV. offer help

   A. I only
   B. I and II
   C. II and III
   D. I, II, III and IV

3. Which of the following is NOT a basic purpose of a professional code of ethics?

   A. To provide a mechanism for professional accountability
   B. To educate professionals about sound conduct
   C. To set standards that will be understood and enforced across all cultures
   D. To serve as a tool for improving practice

4. According to cognitive-behavioral theory, schemas represent a client's

   A. subversive attempts to persist in faulty cognitions
   B. automatic responses
   C. different response patterns
   D. core beliefs and assumptions

5. Objective data found in a client's folder might include

   A. A neighbor's recorded statement about a previous incident
   B. Notes on an interview with his psychotherapist
   C. A work evaluation performed by a supervisor
   D. A summary of previous criminal convictions

6. In the middle phase of a client interview, as a problem is being further explored, the practitioner should spend a considerable amount of time

   A. interpreting behavior
   B. confronting discrepancies
   C. restating or paraphrasing
   D. negotiating a service contract

7. Which of the following statements is TRUE about social work assessment?

   A. It is another term for "goal setting."
   B. It identifies a problem and its potential impact.
   C. It refers to the search for alternative solutions.
   D. It relates to the evaluation of program effectiveness.

8. An agency needs to write a proposal to a private foundation in order to request funding for renovations. It will be necessary for the agency to organize a _____ group.

   A. training
   B. task-focused
   C. recreation
   D. self-help

9. Social exchange theory is based on the idea that people

   A. often attempt to superimpose their own needs onto the desires of others
   B. aim to protect themselves from punishment in relationships
   C. aim to maximize rewards and minimize costs in relationships
   D. exchange rewards with those who are most like themselves

10. Privileged communication typically applies in cases of
    I. marital infidelity, if both spouses are participating in treatment
    II. legal proceedings in which a practitioner is asked to produce client records in court
    III. child abuse or neglect
    IV. client disclosures of personal and sensitive information

    A. I and III
    B. I, II and IV
    C. III and IV
    D. I, II, III and IV

11. During an assessment interview, a practitioner asks questions about the client's customs and traditions. The practitioner is most likely seeking information about the impact of _____ on the client's functioning.

    A. unhealthy patterns
    B. self-talk
    C. interpersonal relationships
    D. cultural diversity

12. Each of the following is true of the intervention phase of social work, EXCEPT that it

    A. is focused on problems
    B. requires interviewing, recording, letter writing, and referral skills
    C. is guided by the principles of self-determination and acceptance
    D. results naturally from a thorough assessment

13. During a client interview, a practitioner is attempting to summarize what the client has just said, but the client gives signs that he does not agree with the summary and intends to interrupt. The practitioner believes it is important for the client to hear how the summary sounds in someone else's words. In order to maintain his turn at speaking, the practitioner may want to

    A. raise an index finger
    B. raise his eyebrows
    C. speak more loudly
    D. stop all accompanying gestures and body movements

14. In Erikson's model of human development, the stage at which a child learns to meet the demands of society is

    A. identity vs. role confusion
    B. industry vs. inferiority
    C. basic trust vs. mistrust
    D. autonomy vs. shame and doubt

15. Generally, controlled experimental designs account for about _____ percent of all social work research.

    A. 5
    B. 20
    C. 35
    D. 55

16. What is the term for a social work process that brings an intervention to a close?

    A. Recognizing success
    B. Integrating gains
    C. Terminating the relationship
    D. Expanding opportunities

17. Which of the following is an example of primary prevention for mental illness?

    A. Crisis intervention
    B. Parent-child communication training
    C. Psychotherapy
    D. Teacher referrals to social workers of children targeted by bullies

18. Which of the following is an example of a closed question?

    A. How do you think you can, as you've said, 'Come more alive?'
    B. Of all the problems we've discussed, which bothers you the most?
    C. What is your relationship with your family?
    D. What kinds of things do you find yourself longing for?

19. Over time, adult personalities are likely to change in each of the following ways, EXCEPT becoming more   19.____

    A. candid
    B. dependable
    C. receptive to the company of others
    D. accepting of hardship

20. Which of the following BEST describes the mission of social work?   20.____

    A. Meeting client needs while influencing social institutions to become more responsive to people
    B. Helping clients negotiate an often complex and difficult network of services
    C. Constantly responding and adapting to social changes in micro and macro environments
    D. Identifying programs and connecting clients to needed services

21. Numerous studies have been conducted to determine which factors in a client/helping professional relationship are consistently related to positive outcomes. Which of the following is/are NOT one of these conditions?   21.____

    A. A relationship analogous to doctor/patient
    B. Empathy and positive regard
    C. A working alliance
    D. Transference and countertransference

22. A person who donates anonymously to a favorite charity is most likely driven by what Maslow called   22.____

    A. intrinsic motivation
    B. extrinsic motivation
    C. affective habituation
    D. self-actualization

23. According to the NASW code of ethics, sexual contact between practitioners and former clients is   23.____

    A. strongly discouraged under any circumstances
    B. discouraged, but considered acceptable if it occurs two years or more after the professional relationship has been terminated
    C. grounds for expulsion from the social work profession
    D. a private matter whose nature is left entirely up to the practitioner and the client

24. During an unstructured interview with a client, a practitioner generally focuses on   24.____

    A. discovering the presenting problem
    B. confronting erroneous self-talk
    C. giving reflective responses that elicit more information
    D. a prescribed list of screening questions

25. Process recording is an assessment technique that is most often used in   25.____

    A. clinical settings
    B. family sculpting

C. one-on-one interviews
D. group sessions

26. The NASW's stance on bartering with clients, rather than simply charging fees for service, includes the opinion that social workers should
    I. participate in barter in only in very limited circumstances
    II. ensure that such arrangements are an accepted practice among professionals in the local community
    III. propose bartering if it is clear the client will be unable to pay for services
    IV. never barter with clients under any circumstances

    A. I only
    B. I and II
    C. I, II and III
    D. IV only

27. Etiquette, customs, and minor regulations are examples of

    A. mores
    B. norms
    C. ethics
    D. folkways

28. A practitioner working in the Adlerian model is likely to use each of the following as an assessment instrument, EXCEPT

    A. personality inventories
    B. ecomaps
    C. lifestyle inventories
    D. early childhood recollections

29. Which of the following information would typically be solicited at the LATEST point in an intake interview?

    A. educational history
    B. family/marital/sexual history
    C. vocational history
    D. past interventions or service requests

30. According to conflict theorists, the "hidden curriculum" of schools

    A. serves to transmit different cultural values
    B. encourages social integration
    C. often results in self-fulfilling prophecy
    D. perpetuates existing social inequalities

31. The high value placed on individual freedom in American society has arguably produced each of the following, EXCEPT

    A. a cultural paradox
    B. an environmental dilemma
    C. unfair economic competition
    D. a *caveat emptor* ("let the buyer beware") approach to the market economy

32. One model of the relationship between helping professionals and clients emphasizes the social influence of professionals in counseling roles. To be effective, practitioners in the counseling role can draw on a power base that arises out of the relationship with the client. In client relationships, the power base that is typically LEAST helpful for the practitioner is known as _____ power.

    A. referent
    B. expert
    C. legitimate
    D. reward

33. In social work, experimental research designs

    A. are the most commonly conducted form of social work research
    B. obligate the researcher to offer a treatment to a control group as soon as possible after the study is terminated
    C. are usually single-system designs
    D. are generally free of ethical concerns if the research is conducted well

34. The term "social stratification" refers to social inequality that is

    A. differential
    B. structured
    C. institutionally sanctioned
    D. imperceptible

35. To a practitioner working from the behavioral perspective, the most important feature of good relationships is

    A. effective coping behaviors
    B. freedom from conflict
    C. complementary needs
    D. well-established boundaries

36. In an initial interview, it is common for clients to

    A. break down emotionally
    B. describe problems in a way that minimizes their own contributions to them
    C. disclose very personal information and emotions
    D. be someone other than the person who has arranged the interview

37. Which of the following is NOT a trend in the use of family approaches in direct social work practice?

    A. Increased attention on the family as an isolated system
    B. Increased attention to family diversity
    C. The use of a variety of social science theoretical approaches
    D. The use of multiple intervention models

38. The process whereby a client's place past feelings or attitudes toward significant people in their lives onto their social work practitioner is known as

    A. transference
    B. denial

C. countertransference
D. projection

39. Social desirability bias often causes people to

    A. make appraisals of others that are based on their social functioning rather than their effectiveness in other roles
    B. attribute their successes to skill, while blaming external factors for failures
    C. modify their responses to surveys or interviews based on what they think are desirable responses
    D. focus on the style of their interactions with others, rather than the substance

40. A social worker attends an evening anniversary party at which she has consumed some alcohol, which she rarely drinks. She doesn't think she is literally drunk, but would acknowledge feeling slightly tipsy and perhaps not in full command of herself. When she arrives at home later, she listens to a message from a client that was left on her answering machine while she was out. The client, with whom she has met several times, is feeling lonely and desperate because of the recent loss of his wife to cancer. The social worker wants to help. She should

    A. return the call immediately and try to counsel the client
    B. return the call immediately and explain that she is unable to help right now, but will call first thing tomorrow
    C. avoid contacting the client until she has recovered her ability to perform up to her usual professional standards and judgement
    D. contact a trusted colleague, give him or her the relevant information, and ask that he or she try to counsel the client over the phone

41. During an assessment interview, a practitioner asks a client: "What kinds of feelings do you have when this happens to you?" The practitioner is trying to identify the _____ associated with the problem.

    A. affect and mood states
    B. secondary gains
    C. overt behaviors or motoric responses
    D. internal dialogue

42. Hospital social workers typically engage in each of the following types of interventions or practice, EXCEPT

    A. crisis intervention
    B. discharge planning
    C. long-term counseling
    D. group work

43. For social work practitioners, symptoms of "burnout" on the job typically include each of the following, EXCEPT

    A. feeling unable to accomplish goals
    B. emotional exhaustion
    C. chronic worry
    D. a feeling of detachment from clients and work

44. When a case manager reaches the point in service coordination during which he makes a referral, he has assumed the role of

   A. evaluator
   B. broker
   C. advocate
   D. planner

45. A practitioner encounters a situation in which his own personal values conflict with a client's. In this instance, the practitioner is expected to engage in

   A. peer review
   B. value suspension
   C. legal consultation
   D. value clarification

46. Among the following American groups, the women who have the greatest risk of HIV infection are

   A. white
   B. African American
   C. Native American
   D. Hispanic

47. The trend in school social work has been a gradual shift toward an emphasis on the _____ perspective.

   A. behavioral
   B. input-based
   C. ecological
   D. psychiatric

48. The success of client-written logs as an assessment tool may depend on the client's motivation to keep a log. Which of the following is LEAST likely to help motivate a client to keep a log?

   A. Establishing a clear rationale or purpose for keeping the log
   B. Establishing negative consequences if the client fails to make log entries
   C. Adapting the log type to the client's abilities to self-monitor
   D. Involving the client in discussing and analyzing the log

49. The social work value of *empathy* is defined as a practitioner's capacity to

   A. imagine oneself in another's situation
   B. feel compassion for a person who is in distress
   C. convince a person that things will get better
   D. make a person recognize his/her own inner strength

50. Focusing on a client's positive assets and strengths during an assessment interview
    I. emphasizes the wholeness of the client system, rather than simply the problematic aspects
    II. gives a practitioner information about potential problems that might arise during an intervention
    III. helps convey to the client that they have internal resources that may prove useful
    IV. risks skewing the effectiveness of an intervention by taking the focus off the presenting problem

    A. I and III
    B. I, II and III
    C. III only
    D. I, II, III and IV

51. A hospital social worker is meeting with an 86-year-old man who suffers from Alzheimer's disease. His symptoms thus far have consisted largely of incidents of forgetfulness, and he has shown no signs of dementia or violence. The client's daughter, who has recently succeeded in having her father grant her a power of attorney over his affairs. When the social worker asks questions of the client, the daughter repeated breaks in and attempts to answer for him, though he appears to be lucid. When the social worker asks to speak to the client alone, the daughter refuses. The social worker should

    A. suspect a case of elder abuse and contact the adult protective services agency to look into it
    B. pretend to leave, and then attempt to interview the man when the daughter leaves the room
    C. suspect that the daughter may have suffered abuse at the hands of her father and adult protective services to look into it
    D. suspect a case of elder abuse and contact local law enforcement authorities

52. Which of the following is a key element of the case management paradigm?

    A. A focus on improving the quality and accessibility of resources
    B. A focus on developing vocational adjustment
    C. The selection of interventions based on empirical research
    D. Rational-emotive therapy

53. Of the following health problems, each affects the elderly to a greater extent than other age groups. The one that leads by the greatest percentage is

    A. cancer
    B. stroke
    C. heart disease
    D. Alzheimer's disease

54. Approximately _____ of all direct practice interventions are terminated because of unanticipated situational factors.

    A. an eighth
    B. a quarter
    C. half
    D. three-quarters

55. Social factors that increase the risk for suicide include each of the following, EXCEPT that the person

    A. lives alone
    B. has repeatedly rejected support
    C. has no ongoing therapeutic relationship
    D. is married

56. Practitioners are generally considered to have an ethical obligation to do each of the following, EXCEPT

    A. remain aware of their own values
    B. seek to learn about the diverse cultural backgrounds of their clients
    C. avoid imposing their values on clients
    D. refer clients whose values strongly differ from their own

57. Studies of young people who join urban gangs suggests that most often, people join gangs because of a need for a(n)

    A. peer group
    B. outlet for pent-up aggression and frustration
    C. surrogate family
    D. vehicle for criminal activity

58. After terminating a working relationship with a social worker, a client joins the local chapter of Alcoholics Anonymous. In doing so, she is attempting to

    A. form new therapeutic relationships
    B. prolong treatment
    C. maintain gains
    D. generalize gains

59. A key concept of narrative therapy is the idea tha

    A. clients often construct one-dimensional stories that don't tell the whole truth
    B. clearly naming a problem or disorder is the first step in solving it
    C. problems are inseparable from the person
    D. interventions are narrowly targeted to "revisions" of specific passages within the story

60. The creation of social service programs typically accomplishes each of the following, EXCEPT

    A. prevention
    B. enhancement
    C. retrenchment
    D. remediation

61. The most significant health problem facing Native Americans today is

    A. tuberculosis
    B. alcoholism
    C. heart disease
    D. diabetes

11 (#2)

62. Which of the following is NOT one of the six "core values" that is cited in the preamble to the NASW's code of ethics?

    A. Service
    B. Confidentiality
    C. Integrity
    D. Importance of human relationships

63. Each of the following is a guideline for a practitioner's participation in crisis intervention procedures, EXCEPT

    A. expressing empathy by saying things such as "I understand"
    B. asking the client to describe the event
    C. letting the client talk for as long as he or she likes without interruption
    D. asking the client to describe his or her reactions and responses

64. A practitioner has begun to work with clients in one-on-one settings. He thinks perhaps self-disclosure would be a good way to establish a solid, caring relationship with his clients. He should remember that in working with clients professionally, there will always be a tension between the competing forces of self-disclosure and

    A. candor
    B. liability
    C. reciprocity
    D. privacy

65. From an ethical standpoint, practitioners may
    I. accept a referral fee
    II. refer a client to a single referral source
    III. use a place of employment, such as a social services agency, to recruit clients for their own private practice
    IV. refer clients only if their problems fall outside the practitioner's area of competence

    A. I and II
    B. II only
    C. II, III and IV
    D. I, II, III and IV

66. According to Carol H. Meyer's widely used model of social work assessment, the first step in the assessment process is

    A. evaluation
    B. inferential thinking
    C. problem definition
    D. exploration

67. What is the term for the theory that explains how people generate explanations for the behaviors of others?

    A. Attribution theory
    B. Stereotyping

C. Thematic apperception
D. Implicit personality theory

68. The most important professional risk associated with amalgamating groups under very broad headings or labels, such as "Asian American," is that

    A. these terms are considered derogatory by many people
    B. most immigrants to this country proudly insist on being referred to as simply "American"
    C. many people resent being folded in to a larger group for the purpose of classification
    D. the label may obscure significant differences in the culture and experiences of individuals or subgroups within the larger category

69. Before entering a social work field placement program, prospective students are ethically entitled to know
    I. dismissal policies and procedures
    II. employment prospects for graduates
    III. the basis for performance evaluation
    IV. names and theoretical perspectives of prospective supervisors

    A. I only
    B. I, II, and III
    C. III only
    D. I, II, III and IV

70. Of the steps involved in recruitment and training at human services organizations, the FIRST typically involves

    A. reference and background checks
    B. posting position announcements
    C. screening interviews
    D. developing a job description

71. During an intake interview, a client generally avoids making eye contact with the practitioner. Averting the eyes in this way is an example of the _____ function of eye contact.

    A. monitoring
    B. expressive
    C. regulatory
    D. cognitive

72. The educational success of American children and youth is highly correlated to

    A. home schooling
    B. regional employment patterns
    C. family values
    D. race and ethnicity

73. Which of the following techniques is a client-centered practitioner MOST likely to use?

    A. Response shaping
    B. Reflection

C. Giving advice
D. Analysis

74. During a meeting with a client who has just ended his marriage after twelve years, the client insists repeatedly that everything is fine. No matter what the practitioner asks or tries to suggest, the response is the same. The client is engaging in the facial management technique known as

A. neutralizing
B. masking
C. intensifying
D. deintensifying

75. A practitioner is considering a dual relationship with a client. Before forming such a relationship, the practitioner should consider
   I. divergent responsibilities
   II. incompatible expectations
   III. the power differential
   IV. referring the client to another practitioner

A. I and II
B. I, II and III
C. II, III and IV
D. I, II, III and IV

KEY (CORRECT ANSWERS)

1. A	16. B	31. A	46. B	61. B
2. C	17. B	32. D	47. C	62. B
3. C	18. B	33. B	48. B	63. A
4. D	19. C	34. B	49. A	64. D
5. D	20. A	35. A	50. B	65. B
6. C	21. A	36. B	51. A	66. D
7. B	22. A	37. A	52. A	67. A
8. B	23. A	38. A	53. C	68. D
9. C	24. C	39. C	54. C	69. B
10. B	25. C	40. C	55. D	70. D
11. D	26. B	41. A	56. D	71. C
12. A	27. D	42. C	57. C	72. D
13. C	28. A	43. C	58. C	73. B
14. B	29. B	44. B	59. A	74. A
15. A	30. D	45. B	60. C	75. B

READING COMPREHENSION
UNDERSTANDING AND INTERPRETING WRITTEN MATERIAL
EXAMINATION SECTION
TEST 1

DIRECTIONS: Each question or incomplete statement is followed by several suggested answers or completions. Select the one that BEST answers the question or completes the statement. *PRINT THE LETTER OF THE CORRECT ANSWER IN THE SPACE AT THE RIGHT.*

Questions 1-5.

DIRECTIONS: Questions 1 through 5 are to be answered SOLELY on the basis of the following paragraph.

In counting the poor, the Social Security Administration has developed two poverty thresholds that designate families as either *poor* or *near poor*. The Administration assumed that the poor would spend the same proportion of income on food as the rest of the population but that, obviously, since their income was smaller, their range of selection would be narrower. In the Low Cost Food Plan, the amount allocated to food from the average expenditure was cut to the minimum that the Agriculture Department said could still provide American families with an adequate diet. This Low Cost Food Plan was used to characterize the *near poor* category, and an even lower Economy Food Plan was used to characterize the *poor* category. The Economy Food Plan was based on $7.00 a person for food each day, assuming that all food would be prepared at home. The Agriculture Department estimates that only about 10 percent of persons spending $7.00 or less for food each day actually were able to get a nutritionally adequate diet.

1. Of the following, the MOST suitable title for the above paragraph would be
   A. THE SUPERIORITY OF THE ECONOMY PLAN OVER THE LOW COST PLAN
   B. THE NEED FOR A NUTRITIONALLY ADEQUATE DIET
   C. FOOD EXPENDITURES OF THE POOR AND THE NEAR POOR
   D. DIET IN THE UNITED STATES

   1.____

2. According to the above paragraph, the Social Security Administration assumed, in setting its poverty levels, that the poor
   A. spend a smaller proportion of income for food than the average non-poor
   B. would not eat in restaurants
   C. as a group includes only those with a nutritionally inadequate diet
   D. spend more money on food than the near poor

   2.____

3. According to the above paragraph, it would be CORRECT to state that the Low Cost Food Plan
   A. is above the minimum set by the Agriculture Department for a nutritionally adequate diet
   B. gives most people a nutritionally inadequate diet
   C. is lower than the Economy Food Plan
   D. represents the amount spent by the near poor

4. As estimated by the Department of Agriculture, the percentage of people spending $7.00 or less a day for food who did NOT get a nutritionally adequate diet was
   A. 100%   B. 90%   C. 10%   D. 0%

5. As used in the above paragraph, the underlined words allocated to mean MOST NEARLY
   A. offered for
   B. assigned to
   C. wasted on
   D. spent on

Questions 6-11.

DIRECTIONS: Questions 6 through 11 are to be answered SOLELY on the basis of the information given in the paragraph below.

Three years ago, the City introduced a program of reduced transit rates for the elderly. It was hoped that this program would increase the travel of the elderly and help them maintain a greater measure of independence. About 600,000 of the 800,000 eligible residents are currently enrolled in the program. To be eligible, a person must be 65 years of age or older and not employed full-time. Riding for reduced fare is permitted between 10:00 A.M. and 4:00 P.M. and between 7:00 P.M. and Midnight on weekdays, and 24 hours a day on Saturdays, Sundays, and holidays.

In a City university study, based on a sampling of 728 enrollees interviewed, it was learned that 51 percent are able to travel more and 30.8 percent had been able to save enough money to make a noticeable difference in their budgets as a result of the reduced-fare program.

It has been recommended that reduced-fare programs be extended to encourage the use of transit lines in off hours by other groups such as the poor, the very young, housewives, and the physically handicapped. To implement this recommendation, it would be necessary for the Federal government to increase transit subsidies.

6. Which one of the following titles would be the BEST for the above passage?
   A. A PROGRAM OF REDUCED TRANSIT RATES FOR THE ELDERLY
   B. RECOMMENDATIONS FOR EXTENDING PROGRAMS FOR THE ELDERLY
   C. CITY UNIVERSITY STUDY ON THE RELATIONSHIP OF AGE AND TRAVEL
   D. ELIGIBILITY REQUIREMENTS FOR THE REDUCED RATE PROGRAM

3 (#1)

7. Approximately what percentage of the eligible residents is currently enrolled in the reduced-fare program?   7.____
   A. 25%   B. 50%   C. 65%   D. 75%

8. Which one of the following persons is NOT eligible for the reduced-fare program?   8.____
   A
   A. woman, age 67, employed part-time as a stenographer
   B. handicapped man, age 62
   C. blind man, age 66, employed part-time as a transcribing typist
   D. housewife, age 70

9. At which one of the following times would the reduced-fare NOT be permitted for an eligible elderly person?   9.____
   A. Sunday, 6:00 P.M.
   B. Christmas Day, 2:00 A.M.
   C. Tuesday, 9:00 A.M.
   D. Thursday, 8:00 P.M.

10. Of the 728 enrollees interviewed in the City university study of the reduced-fare program, it was found that   10.____
    A. the majority traveled more and saved money at the same time
    B. more than half traveled less and, therefore, saved money
    C. about half traveled more and about one-third saved money
    D. the majority saved money but traveled the same rate as before

11. According to the above passage, what would be necessary to extend the reduced-fare program to other groups of people?   11.____
    A. Increasing the eligible age to 68
    B. Reducing the hours when half-fare is permitted
    C. Increasing the fare for other riders
    D. Increasing the transit subsidies by the Federal government

Questions 12-14.

DIRECTIONS: Questions 12 through 14 are to be answered SOLELY on the basis of the following passage.

Local public welfare agencies, in general, recognize that more time is required for Aid to Dependent Children cases and General Assistance cases than for Old Age Assistance cases, and that the intensive work required in Child Welfare Service cases necessitates special planning with regard to limiting caseloads for workers to prevent their carrying too large a number of cases. A General Assistance case often includes several persons, while Old Age Assistance cases are on an individual basis. Although the average cost of a case per month has continued to increase for all assistance programs, these programs have retained their relative cost positions. The average monthly cost of a case has been lowest for Aid to the Aged, followed, in ascending order, by Aid to the Blind, Aid to Dependent Children, and General Assistance, with the cost per case of the last mentioned program averaging more than four times that for Aid to the Aged. On the other hand, the proportion of Aid to the Aged cases is rising while the percentage of General Assistance cases is declining.

12. Some types of cases require more time or more intensive work than others. The one of the following statements which MOST accurately illustrates this point, according to the above paragraph, is:

    A. Aid to the Blind cases often included several persons and, therefore, are very time-consuming, while Old Age Assistance cases require intensive casework
    B. Aid to Dependent Children cases often involve complicated situations and, therefore, require intensive casework, while Aid to the Blind cases are extremely time-consuming
    C. Old Age Assistance cases are relatively less time-consuming, while Child Welfare Service cases entail detailed casework
    D. Old Age Assistance cases are time-consuming, while General Assistance cases are comparatively simple

    12.____

13. If a public welfare official were to set up several caseloads, with each caseload containing the same total number of cases but with a varying number in each of the different types of assistance, the caseload which would MOST likely require the GREATEST expenditure of time would be the one with a majority of

    A. Aid to the Blind cases and Aid to Dependent Children cases
    B. General Assistance cases and Aid to Dependent Children cases
    C. Old Age Assistance cases and Aid to the Blind cases
    D. Old Age Assistance cases and General Assistance cases

    13.____

14. According to the above paragraph, the one of the following statements which is the MOST accurate with regard to the cost of welfare services is that

    A. the average monthly cost for each Aid to Dependent Children case was higher than for each Aid to the Blind case but lower than for each Aid to the Aged case
    B. the cost per case for General Assistance has risen four times as fast as the cost per case for Aid to the Aged
    C. there has been a decrease in the proportion of General Assistance cases, but the cost per case in this category has increased
    D. more than four times as much money was spent in total for all the cases in the General Assistance program than for those in the Aid to the Aged program

    14.____

Questions 15-17.

DIRECTIONS: Questions 15 through 17 are to be answered SOLELY on the basis of the following passage.

Aid to dependent children shall be given to a parent or other relative as herein specified for the benefit of a child or children under sixteen years of age or of a minor or minors between sixteen and eighteen years of age if in the judgment of the administrative agency: (1) the granting of an allowance will be in the interest of such child or minor, and (2) the parent or other relative is a fit person to bring up such child or minor so that his physical, mental, and moral well-being will be safeguarded, and (3) aid is necessary to enable such parent or other relative to do so, and (4) such child or minor is a resident of the state on the date of application for aid, and (5) such minor between sixteen and eighteen years of age is regularly attending school in accordance with the regulations of the department. An allowance may be granted for the aid of such child or minor who has been deprived of parental support or care by reason of the death, continued absence from the home, or physical or mental incapacity of a parent, and who is living with his father, mother, grandfather, grandmother, brother, sister, stepfather, stepmother, stepbrother, stepsister, uncle, or aunt. In making such allowances, consideration shall be given to the ability of the relative making application and of any other relatives to support and are for or to contribute to the support and care of such child or minor. In making all such allowances, it shall be made certain that the religious faith of the child or minor shall be preserved and protected.

15. The above passage is concerned PRIMARILY with 15.____
    A. the financial ability of persons applying for public assistance
    B. compliance on the part of applicants with the *settlement* provisions of the law
    C. the fitness of parents or other relatives to bring up physically, mentally, or morally delinquent children between the ages of sixteen and eighteen
    D. eligibility for aid to dependent children

16. On the basis of the above passage, the MOST accurate of the following 16.____
    statements is:
    A. Mary Doe, mother of John, age 18, is entitled to aid for her son if he is attending school regularly
    B. Evelyn Stowe, mother of Eleanor, age 13, is not entitled to aid for Eleanor if she uses her home for immoral purposes
    C. Ann Roe, cousin of Helen, age 14, is entitled to aid for Helen if the latter is living with her
    D. Peter Moe, uncle of Henry, age 15, is not entitled to aid for Henry if the latter is living with him

17. The above passage is PROBABLY an excerpt of the 17.____
    A. Administrative Code   B. Social Welfare Law
    C. Federal Security Act   D. City Charter

Questions 18-20.

DIRECTIONS: Questions 18 through 20 are to be answered SOLELY on the basis of the information contained in the following passage.

On the state level, in an effort to obtain better administration and delivery of services in the Medicaid program, the Governor has appointed a committee to advise the State Commissioner of Social Welfare on medical care services. Included on this committee are representatives of the medical, dental, pharmaceutical, nursing, and social work professions, as well as persons representing the fields of mental health, home health agencies, nursing homes, schools of health science, public health and welfare administrations, and the general public. Several of the committee members are physicians in private practice who represent and uphold the interests of the private physicians who care for Medicaid patients.

The committee not only makes recommendations on the standards, quality, and costs of medical services, personnel, and facilities, but also helps identify unmet needs, and assists in long-range planning, evaluation, and utilization of services. It advises, as requested, on administrative and fiscal matters, and also interprets the programs and goals to professional groups.

On the city level, representatives of the county medical societies of the city meet periodically with Medicaid administrators to discuss problems and consider proposals. It is hoped that the county medical societies will assume the responsibility of informing citizens as to where they can receive medical care under Medicaid.

18. Based on information in the above passage, it can be inferred that the group on the advisory committee likely to be LEAST objective in their recommendations would be the representatives of the
    A. public health and welfare administrations
    B. general public
    C. private physicians
    D. schools of health science

19. The above passage suggests that a problem with the Medicaid program is that
    A. the Mayor has not appointed a committee to work with the City Commissioner of Social Services
    B. many people do not know where they can go to obtain medical care under the program
    C. the county medical societies do not meet often enough with the Medicaid program administrators
    D. citizens do not take the initiative to seek out sources of available medical care under the program

20. According to the above passage, the Governor's objective in appointing the advisory committee was to
    A. obtain more cooperation from the county medical societies
    B. get the members of the committee to provide medical care services to Medicaid recipients
    C. help improve the Medicaid program in all its aspects, including administration and provision of services
    D. persuade a greater number of private physicians and other health care professionals to accept Medicaid patients

Questions 21-25.

DIRECTIONS: Questions 21 through 25 are to be answered SOLELY on the basis of the following passage.

Any person who is living in the city and is otherwise eligible may be granted public assistance whether or not he has state residence. However, since the city does not contribute to the cost of assistance granted to persons who are without state residence, the cases of all recipients must be formally identified as to whether or not each member of the household has state residence.

To acquire state residence, a person must have resided in the state continuously for one year. Such residence is not lost unless the person is out of the state continuously for a period of one year or longer. Continuous residence does not include any period during which the individual is a patient in a hospital, an inmate of a public institution or of an incorporated private institution, a resident on a military reservation or a minor residing in a boarding home while under the care of an authorized agency. Receipt of public assistance does not prevent a person from acquiring state residence. State residence, once acquired, is not lost because of absence from the state while a person is serving in the United States Armed Forces or the Merchant Marine; nor does a member of the family of such a person lose state residence while living with or near that person in these circumstances.

Each person, regardless of age, acquires or loses state residence as an individual. There is no derivative state residence except for an infant at the time of birth. He is deemed to have state residence if he is in the custody of both parents and either one of them has state residence, or if the parent having custody of his has state residence.

21. According to the above passage, an infant is deemed to have state residence at the time of his birth if
   A. he is born in the state but neither of his parents is a resident
   B. he is in the custody of only one parent, who is not a resident but his other parent is a resident
   C. his brother and sister are residents
   D. he is in the custody of both his parents but only one of them is a resident

22. The Jones family consists of five members. Jack and Mary Jones have lived in New York State continuously for the past eighteen months after having lived in Ohio since they were born. Of their three children, one was born ten months ago and has been in the custody of his parents since birth. Their second child lived in Ohio until six months ago and then moved in with his parents. Their third child had never lived in New York until he moved with his parents to New York eighteen months ago. However, he entered the Armed Forces one month later and has not lived in New York since that time. Based on the above passage, how many members of the Jones family are New York State residents?
   A. 2   B. 3   C. 4   D. 5

23. Assuming that each of the following individuals has lived continuously in the state for the past year, and has never previously lived in the state, which one of them is a state resident?
    A. Jack Salinas, who has been an inmate in a state correctional facility for six months of the year
    B. Fran Johnson, who has lived on an Army base for the entire year
    C. Arlene Snyder, who married a non-resident during the past year
    D. Gary Phillips, who was a patient in a Veterans Administration Hospital for the entire year

24. The above passage implies that the reason for determining whether or not a recipient of public assistance is a state resident is that
    A. the cost of assistance for non-residents is not a city responsibility
    B. non-residents living in the city are not eligible for public assistance
    C. recipients of public assistance are barred from acquiring state residence
    D. the city is responsible for the full cost of assistance to recipients who are residents

25. Assume that the Rollins household in the city consists of six members at the present time – Anne Rollins, her three children, her aunt, and her uncle. Anne Rollins and one of her children moved to the city seven months ago. Neither of them had previously lived in the state. Her other two children have lived in the city continuously for the past two years, as has her aunt. Anne Rollins' uncle had lived in the city continuously for many years until two years ago. He then entered the Armed Forces and has returned to the city within the past month. Based on the above passage, how many members of the Rollins' household are state residents?
    A. 2   B. 3   C. 4   D. 6

KEY (CORRECT ANSWERS)

1. C
2. B
3. D
4. B
5. B

6. A
7. D
8. B
9. C
10. C

11. D
12. C
13. B
14. C
15. D

16. B
17. B
18. C
19. B
20. C

21. D
22. B
23. C
24. A
25. C

TEST 2

DIRECTIONS: Each question or incomplete statement is followed by several suggested answers or completions. Select the one that BEST answers the question or completes the statement. *PRINT THE LETTER OF THE CORRECT ANSWER IN THE SPACE AT THE RIGHT.*

Questions 1-4.

DIRECTIONS: Questions 1 through 4 are to be answered SOLELY on the basis of the following passage.

The loss of control over the use of a drug — called addiction where there is both physical and psychological dependence, and habituation where there is psychological dependence without physical dependence — is, regardless of the particular drug involved, a disease. Both chronic alcoholism and narcotics addiction are usually recognized as diseases.

It is inappropriate to invoke the criminal process against persons who have lost control over the use of dangerous drugs solely because these persons are drug users. Once a person has lost control over his use of drugs, the existence of offenses such as drug use or simple possession will not deter his use. Having lost control, he cannot choose to conform his conduct to the requirements of the law by refraining from use. He is non-deterrable.

Admittedly, there may be times before a person loses control over his use of drugs when he did have a choice of whether to use or not to use, or to stop using. Because of this, punishing him for use or simple possession would not offend the principle that to be punishable conduct must be a result of free choice.

1. Of the following, the MOST suitable title for the above passage is 1.____
   A. DRUG ADDICTION
   B. DRUG ABUSE AND PUNISHMENT
   C. HABITUATION AND THE CRIMINAL PROCESS
   D. PREVENTING DRUG-RELATED CRIME

2. According to the above passage, addiction and habituation are 2.____
   A. identical in meaning because both are diseases related to drug use
   B. identical in meaning because both involve dependence on drugs
   C. similar to the extent that both involve physical dependence on a drug
   D. similar to the extent that both involve psychological dependence on a drug

3. According to the above passage, punishing drug abusers would be justifiable ONLY if their behavior were 3.____
   A. elective   B. non-deterrable
   C. chronic   D. dangerous

4. According to the above passage, punishing a person for simple possession of drugs is 4.____
   A. appropriate under certain circumstances
   B. inappropriate because the person could not have acted otherwise
   C. necessary for the protection of society
   D. unfair because it penalizes past conduct

Questions 5-8.

DIRECTIONS: Questions 5 through 8 are to be answered SOLELY on the basis of the following passage.

The usually explanation for drunken behavior is that alcohol, which is a physiological depressant, impairs reasoning and inhibition powers before it depresses the ability to act and to express emotion.

The purely physiological effects of alcohol are very much like of those of fatigue. Individual personality and social and cultural influences apparently greatly determine how these effects are reflected in changed behavior as alcohol is consumed. Therefore, one can assert that alcohol alone does not cause drunken behavior; rather, drunken behavior expresses personal character, cultural traditions, and social circumstances, as they influence a person's reactions to the physiological effects of alcohol on his body.

For some people, and in some circumstances, these personal, cultural, and social factors may readily express themselves as criminal behavior. The most obvious case, of course, is public drunkenness.

The exact relationship between various crimes and various stages of intoxication is not completely known. G.M. Scott believes that the moderate stages of intoxication are the ones usually associated with crime since the latter states of intoxication make performance of crime impossible. Dr. Banay found that many drunks are drawn into crime not only by the need of money to replace wages that drinking prevents them from earning, but also by their increased irritability and pugnacity. He discovered that most of the sex offenses for which offenders are committed to state prisons show a relation between alcohol and the crime and that the average sex case is a clear-cut illustration of the hypothesis that alcohol covers up an underlying condition and that some dormant tendency is either brought to the surface or aggravated by alcohol.

In addition to drunken behavior resulting in criminal acts, it is also connected to several other important social problems. Reference can be made particularly to dependency, unemployment, desertion, divorce, vagrancy, and suicide. For all of these social ills, alcohol acts as the physiological depressing agent which influences one's deviation from normative behavior.

5. Discussions of intoxication customarily state that alcohol 5.____
   A. initially affects the analytic faculty
   B. initially affects the ability to express feelings
   C. reduces the desire for money
   D. stimulates perception of the true nature of one's condition

6. Which one of the following hypotheses would Dr. Banay MOST likely support?
   A. The casual drinker is LESS likely to commit a crime than the chronic drinker.
   B. An aggressive drunk is LIKELY to have aggressive tendencies when not under the influence of alcohol.
   C. The UNDERLYING cause of most sex offenses is excessive drinking.
   D. There is NO connection between cultural background and drunken behavior.

7. The title BEST suited for the above passage is
   A. HOW ALCOHOL INFLUENCES POTENTIAL SEXUAL OFFENDERS
   B. STAGES OF INTOXICATION
   C. THE ROLE OF ALCOHOLIC CONSUMPTION IN HUMAN BEHAVIOR
   D. THE RELATIONSHIP BETWEEN ALCOHOL AND EMOTION

8. The writer implies that
   A. a desire to destroy oneself is a frequent side effect of drinking intoxicating liquors
   B. a person who is drunk may find it easier to kill himself
   C. there is a pattern of drinking behavior in the background of most suicides
   D. there is no relationship between the problems of drinking and suicide

Questions 9-11.

DIRECTIONS: Questions 9 through 11 are to be answered SOLELY on the basis of the following paragraph.

A substantial source of opposition to legalizing heroin is those people who are convinced that this idea is simply another form of social and economic injustice. Instead of getting at the fundamental causes of addiction, they say, the result will be to turn hundreds of young addicts into the living dead.

9. According to the above paragraph, opposition to legalizing heroin is based, in part, on the belief that
   A. some addicts will become walking dead people
   B. the problem is entirely one of educating individuals
   C. the pushers will simply turn to other criminal activities
   D. the root causes of addiction are still mysterious

10. Which of the following treatment approaches would the author of the above paragraph be MOST likely to oppose?
    A. Ambulatory detoxification   B. Methadone maintenance
    C. Drug-free therapeutic community D. Youth intervention program

11. As used in the above paragraph, the underlined word substantial means MOST NEARLY
    A. known   B. large   C. strange   D. unanimous

Questions 12-16.

DIRECTIONS: Questions 12 through 16 are to be answered SOLELY on the basis of the following paragraph.

In the last dozen years or so, there has emerged an argument which obviously has a certain persuasiveness among young people: that drugs are being used, not as an expression of antisocial behavior or for escape, but to define a different, anti-establishment culture. Drugs can, of course, be used that way; it's very possible to have a youth culture that uses drugs as a norm. But it's also possible to have a youth culture that is opposed to using drugs as a norm. For example, in China, around 1910, a very effective campaign against opium was led largely by students who felt that the use of drugs was the reason China had suffered so much at the hands of the Western powers.

12. According to the above paragraph, the Chinese students opposed the use of opium because
    A. it contradicted Chinese religious values
    B. it interfered with their studies
    C. they believed it weakened their country
    D. the Western powers encouraged addiction

13. The writer of the above paragraph seems to believe that there is no necessary connection between
    A. escapism and culture
    B. norms and values
    C. students and politics
    D. youth and drugs

14. According to the above paragraph, it is possible to have a youth culture that considers the use of drugs
    A. completely acceptable
    B. legally defensible
    C. morally uplifting
    D. physically beneficial

15. The underlined word emerged means MOST NEARLY
    A. come into view
    B. gone through
    C. required to be
    D. responded quickly

16. As used in the above paragraph, the underlined word norm means MOST NEARLY
    A. argument of explanation
    B. error or mistake
    C. pleasure or reward
    D. rule or average

Questions 17-20.

DIRECTIONS: Questions 17 through 20 are to be answered SOLELY on the basis of the following paragraph.

Alcoholics are to be found in both sexes, in every major religious and racial group, and at all socio-economic levels. What they share in common are psychiatric problems which they seek to ease or dull through alcohol. Ideally, every heavy drinker should be subjected to intensive psychiatric therapy. Unfortunately, even psychiatric treatment is not always successful, and in any case the nation has allocated neither the funds nor the personnel nor the facilities that would be required for such a massive therapeutic effort.

17. According to the above paragraph, national priorities in connection with psychiatric treatment for alcoholism do NOT provide for
    A. fair and impartial treatment
    B. large-scale programs
    C. proper religious values
    D. strict laws against alcoholism

17.____

18. According to the above paragraph, alcoholics are MOST likely to be
    A. emotionally disturbed
    B. ultimately curable
    C. unable to function
    D. under medical care

18.____

19. As used in the above paragraph, the underlined word intensive means MOST NEARLY
    A. concentrated   B. modern   C. prompt   D. specialized

19.____

20. As used in the above paragraph, the underlined word allocated means MOST NEARLY
    A. assigned   B. conserved   C. desired   D. recognized

20.____

Questions 21-25.

DIRECTIONS: Questions 21 through 25 are to be answered SOLELY on the basis of the following paragraph.

The practice of occasionally adulterating marijuana complicates analysis of the effects of marijuana use in non-controlled settings. Behavioral changes which are attributed to marijuana may actually derive from the adulterants or from the interaction of tetrahydrocannabinols and adulterants. Similarly, in today's society, marijuana is often used simultaneously or sequentially with other psycho-active drugs. When drug interactions occur, the simultaneous presence of two or more drugs in the body can exert effects which are more than that which would result from the simple addition of the effects of each drug used separately. Thus, the total behavioral response may be greater than the sum of its parts. For example, if a given dose of marijuana induced two units of perceptual distortion, and a certain dose of LSD given alone induced two units of perceptual distortion, the simultaneous administration of these doses of marijuana and LSD may induce not four but five units of perceptual distortion.

21. According to the above paragraph, the concurrent presence of two drugs in the body can
    A. compound the effects of both drugs
    B. reduce perceptual distortion
    C. simulate psychotic symptoms
    D. be highly toxic

22. Based on the above paragraph, it is MOST reasonable to assume that tetrahydrocannabinols are
    A. habit-forming substances
    B. components of marijuana
    C. similar to quinine or milk-sugar
    D. used as adulterants

23. Based on the above paragraph, it is MOSTS reasonable to state that marijuana is
    A. most affected by adulterants when used as a psycho-active drug
    B. erroneously considered to be less harmful than other drugs
    C. frequently used in connection with other mind-affecting drugs
    D. occasionally used as an adjunct to LSD in order to reduce bad reactions

24. As used in the above paragraph, the underlined word attributed means MOST NEARLY
    A. originally unsuspected
    B. identical in action
    C. known as a reason
    D. ascribed by way of cause

25. As used in the above paragraph, the underlined word induced means MOST NEARLY
    A. caused   B. projected   C. required   D. displayed

KEY (CORRECT ANSWERS)

1.	B	11.	B
2.	D	12.	C
3.	A	13.	D
4.	A	14.	A
5.	A	15.	A
6.	B	16.	D
7.	C	17.	B
8.	B	18.	A
9.	A	19.	A
10.	B	20.	A

21. A
22. B
23. C
24. D
25. A

PREPARING WRITTEN MATERIAL

PARAGRAPH REARRANGEMENT
COMMENTARY

The sentences that follow are in scrambled order. You are to rearrange them in proper order and indicate the letter choice containing the correct answer at the space at the right.

Each group of sentences in this section is actually a paragraph presented in scrambled order. Each sentence in the group has a place in that paragraph; no sentence is to be left out. You are to read each group of sentences and decide upon the best order in which to put the sentences so as to form a well-organized paragraph.

The questions in this section measure the ability to solve a problem when all the facts relevant to its solution are not given.

More specifically, certain positions of responsibility and authority require the employee to discover connection between events sometimes, apparently, unrelated. In order to do this, the employee will find it necessary to correctly infer that unspecified events have probably occurred or are likely to occur. This ability becomes especially important when action must be taken on incomplete information.

Accordingly, these questions require competitors to choose among several suggested alternatives, each of which presents a different sequential arrangement of the events. Competitors must choose the MOST logical of the suggested sequences.

In order to do so, they may be required to draw on general knowledge to infer missing concepts or events that are essential to sequencing the given events. Competitors should be careful to infer only what is essential to the sequence. The plausibility of the wrong alternatives will always require the inclusion of unlikely events or of additional chains of events which are NOT essential to sequencing the given events.

It's very important to remember that you are looking for the best of the four possible choices, and that the best choice of all may not even be one of the answers you're given to choose from.

There is no one right way to solve these problems. Many people have found it helpful to first write out the order of the sentences, as they would have arranged them, on their scrap paper before looking at the possible answers. If their optimum answer is there, this can save them some time. If it isn't, this method can still give insight into solving the problem. Others find it most helpful to just go through each of the possible choices, contrasting each as they go along. You should use whatever method feels comfortable and works for you.

While most of these types of questions are not that difficult, we've added a higher percentage of the difficult type, just to give you more practice. Usually there are only one or two questions on this section that contain such subtle distinctions that you're unable to answer confidently. And you then may find yourself stuck deciding between two possible choices, neither of which you're sure about.

PREPARING WRITTEN MATERIAL
PARAGRAPH REARRANGEMENT
EXAMINATION SECTION
TEST 1

DIRECTIONS: The following groups of sentences need to be arranged in an order that makes sense. Select the letter preceding the sequence that represents the best sentence order. *PRINT THE LETTER OF THE CORRECT ANSWER IN THE SPACE AT THE RIGHT.*

1. I. The ostrich egg shell's legendary toughness makes it an excellent substitute for certain types of dishes or dinnerware, and in parts of Africa ostrich shells are cut and decorated for use as containers for water.
    II. Since prehistoric times, people have used the enormous egg of the ostrich as a part of their diet, a practice which has required much patience and hard work—to hard boil an ostrich egg takes about four hours.
    III. Opening the egg's shell, which is rock hard and nearly an inch thick, requires heavy tools, such as a saw or chisel; from inside, a baby ostrich must use a hornlike projection on its beak as a miniature pick-axe to escape from the egg.
    IV. The offspring of all higher-order animals originate from single egg cells that are carried by mothers, and most of these eggs are relatively small, often microscopic.
    V. The egg of the African ostrich, however, weighs a massive thirty pounds, making it the largest single cell on earth, and a common object of human curiosity and wonder.

    The BEST order is:
    A. V, IV, I, II, III
    B. I, IV, V, III, II
    C. IV, II, III, V, I
    D. IV, V, II, III, I

    1.____

2. I. Typically only a few feet high on the open sea, individual tsunami have been known to circle the entire globe two or three times if their progress is not interrupted, but are not usually dangerous until they approach the shallow water that surrounds land masses.
    II. Some of the most terrifying and damaging hazards caused by earthquakes are tsunami, which were once called "tidal waves"—a poorly chosen name, since these waves have nothing to do with tides.
    III. Then a wave, slowed by the sudden drag on the lower part of its moving water column, will pile upon itself, sometimes reaching a height of over 100 feet.
    IV. Tsunami (Japanese for "great harbor wave") are seismic waves that are caused by earthquakes near oceanic trenches, and once triggered, can travel up to 600 miles an hour on the open ocean.
    V. A land-shoaling tsunami is capable of extraordinary destruction; some tsunami have deposited large boats miles inland, washed out two-foot-thick seawalls, and scattered locomotive trains over long distances.

    The BEST order is:
    A. IV, I, III, II, V
    B. I, III, IV, II, V
    C. V, I, III, II, IV
    D. II, IV, I, III, V

    2.____

103

3.
   I. Soon, by the 1940s, jazz was the most popular type of music among American intellectuals and college students.
   II. In the early days of jazz, it was considered "lowdown" music, or music that was played only in rough, disreputable bars and taverns.
   III. However, jazz didn't take too long to develop from early ragtime melodies into more complex, sophisticated forms, such as Charlie Parker's "bebop" style of jazz.
   IV. After charismatic band leaders such as Duke Ellington and Count Basie brought jazz to a larger audience, and jazz continued to evolve into more complicated forms, white audiences began to accept and even to enjoy the new American art form.
   V. Many white Americans, who then dictated the tastes of society, were wary of music that was played almost exclusively in black clubs in the poorer sections of cities and towns.
   The BEST order is:
   A. V, IV, III, II, I   B. II, V, III, IV, I   C. IV, V, III, I, II   D. I, II, IV, III, V

3.____

4.
   I. Then, hanging in a windless place, the magnetized end of the needle would always point to the south.
   II. The needle could then be balanced on the rim of a cup, or the edge of a fingernail, but this balancing act was hard to maintain, and the needle often fell off.
   III. Other needles would point to the north, and it was important for any traveler finding his way with a compass to remember which kind of magnetized needle he was carrying.
   IV. To make some of the earliest compasses in recorded history, ancient Chinese "magicians" would rub a needle with a piece of magnetized iron called a lodestone.
   V. A more effective method of keeping the needle free to swing with its magnetic pull was to attach a strand of silk to the center of the needle with a tiny piece of wax.
   The BEST order is:
   A. IV, II, V, I, III   B. IV, III, V, II, I   C. IV, V, II, I, III   D. IV, I, III, V, II

4.____

5.
   I The now-famous first mate of the *H.M.S. Bounty*, Fletcher Christian, founded one of the world's most peculiar civilizations in 1790.
   II. The men knew they had just committed a crime for which they could be hanged, so they set sail for Pitcairn, a remote, abandoned island in the far eastern region of the Polynesian archipelago, accompanied by twelve Polynesian women and six men.
   III. In a mutiny that has become legendary, Christian and the others forced Captain Bligh into a lifeboat and set him adrift off the coast of Tonga in April of 1789.
   IV. In early 1790, the *Bounty* landed at Pitcairn Island, where the men lived out the rest of their lives and founded an isolated community which to this day includes direct descendants of Christian and the other Crewmen.

5.____

V. The *Bounty*, commanded by Captain William Bligh, was in the middle of a global voyage, and Christian and his shipmates had come to the conclusion that Bligh was a reckless madman who would lead them to their deaths unless they took the ship from him.

The BEST order is:

A. IV, V, III, II, I   B. I, III, V, II, IV   C. I, V, III, II, IV   D. III, I, V, IV, II

6.
I. But once the vines had been led to make orchids, the flowers had to be carefully hand-pollinated, because unpollinated orchids usually lasted less than a day, wilting and dropping off the vine before it had even become dark.
II. The Totonac farmers discovered that looping a vine back around once it reached a five-foot height on its host tree would cause the vine to flower.
III. Though they knew how to process the fruit pods and extract vanilla's flavoring agent, the Totonacs also knew that a wild vanilla vine did not produce abundant flowers or fruit.
IV. Wild vines climbed along the trunks and canopies of trees, and this constant upward growth diverted most of the vine's energy to making leaves instead of the orchid flowers that once pollinated, would produce the flavorful pods.
V. Hundreds of years before vanilla became a prized food flavoring in Europe and the Western World, the Totonac Indians of the Mexican Gulf Coast were skilled cultivators of the vanilla vine, whose fruit they literally worshipped as a goddess.

The BEST order is:

A. II, III, IV, I, V   B. II, IV, III, I, V   C. V, III, IV, II, I   D. III, IV, I, II, V

7.
I. Once airborne, the spider is at the mercy of the air currents—usually the spider takes a brief journey, traveling close to the ground, but some have been found in air samples collected as high as 10,000 feet, or been reported landing on ships far out at sea.
II. Once a young spider has hatched, it must leave the environment into which it was born as quickly as possible, in order to avoid competing with its hundreds of brothers and sisters for food.
III. The silk rises into warm air currents, and as soon as the pull feels adequate the spider lets go and drifts up into the air, suspended from the silk strand in the same way that a person might parasail.
IV. To help young spiders do this, many species have adapted a practice known as "aerial dispersal," or, in common speech, "ballooning."
V. A spider that wants to leave its surroundings quickly will climb to the top of a grass system or twig, face into the wind, and aim its back end into the air, releasing a long stream of silk from the glands near the tip of its abdomen.

The BEST order is:

A. V, IV, II, III, I   B. V, II, IV, I, III   C. II, V, IV, III, I   D. II, IV, V, III, I

8.   I. For about a year, Tycho worked at a castle in Prague with a scientist named Johannes Kepler, but their association was cut short by another argument that drove Kepler out of the castle, to later develop, on his own, the theory of planetary orbits.
   II. Tycho found life without a nose embarrassing, so he made a new nose for himself out of silver, which reportedly remained glued to his face for the rest of his life.
   III. Tycho Brahe, the 17th-century Danish astronomer, is today more famous for his odd and arrogant personality than for any contribution he has made to our knowledge of the stars and planets.
   IV. Early in his career, as a student at Rostock University, Tycho got into an argument with another student about who was the better mathematician, and the two became so angry that the argument turned into a sword fight, during which Tycho's nose was sliced off.
   V. Later in his life, Tycho's arrogance may have kept him from playing a part in one of the greatest astronomical discoveries in history: the elliptical orbits of the solar system's planets.
   The BEST order is:
   A. I, IV, II, III, V   B. IV, II, III, V, I   C. IV, II, I, III, V   D. III, IV, II, V, I

9.   I. The processionaries are so used to this routine that if a person picks up the end of a silk line and brings it back to the origin—creating a closed circle—the caterpillars may travel around and around for days, sometimes starving or freezing, without changing course.
   II. Rather than relying on sight or sound, the other caterpillars, who are lined up end-to-end behind the leader, travel to and from their nests by walking on this silk line, and each will reinforce it by laying down its own marking line as it passes over.
   III. In order to insure the safety of individuals, the processionary caterpillar nests in a tree with dozens of other caterpillars, and at night, when it is safest, they all leave together in search of food.
   IV. The processionary caterpillar of the European continent is a perfect illustration of how much some inspect species rely on instinct in their daily routines.
   V. As they leave their nests, the processionaries form a single-file line behind a leader who spins and lays out a silk line to mark the chosen path.
   The BEST order is:
   A. IV, III, V, II, I   B. III, V, IV, II, I   C. III, V, II, I, IV   D. IV, V, III, I, II

10. I. Often, the child is also given a handcrafted walker or push cart, to provide support for its first upright explorations.
   II. In traditional Indian families, a child's first steps are celebrated as a ceremonial event, rooted in ancient myth.
   III. These carts are often intricately designed to resemble the chariot of Krishna, an important figure in Indian mythology.
   IV. The sound of these anklet bells is intended to mimic the footsteps of the legendary child Rama, who is celebrated in devotional songs throughout India.

V. When the child's parents see that the child is ready to begin walking, they will fit it with specially designed ankle bracelets, adorned with gently ringing bells.

The BEST order is:

A. II, III, IV, I, V   B. II, V, III, I, IV   C. V, IV, I, III, II   D. V, III, II, I, IV

11. I. The settlers planted Osage oranges all across Middle America, and today long lines and rectangles of Osage orange trees can still be seen on the prairies, running along the former boundaries of farms that no longer exist.
    II. After trying sod walls and water-filled ditches with no success, American farmers began to look for a plant that was adaptable to prairie weather, and that could be trimmed into a hedge that was "pig-tight, horse-high, and bull-strong."
    III. The tree, so named because it bore a large (but inedible) fruit the size of an orange, was among the sturdiest and hardiest of American trees, and was prized among Native Americans for the strength and flexibility of bows which were made from its wood.
    IV. The first people to practice agriculture on the American flatlands were faced with an important problem: what would they use to fence their land in a place that was almost entirely without trees or rocks?
    V. Finally, an Illinois farmer brought the settlers a tree that was native to the land between the Red and Arkansas rivers, a tree called the Osage orange.

    The BEST order is:

    A. II, I, V, III, IV   B. I, II, III, IV, V   C. IV, II, V, III, I   D. IV, II, I, III, V

12. I. After about ten minutes of such spirited and complicated activity, the head dancer is free to make up his or her own movements while maintaining the interest of the New Year's crowd.
    II. The dancer will then perform a series of leg kicks, while at the same time operating the lion's mouth with his own hand and moving the ears and eyes by means of a string which is attached to the dancer's own mouth.
    III. The most difficult role of this dance belongs to the one who controls the lion's head; this person must lead all the other "parts" of the lion through the choreographed segments of the dance.
    IV. The head dancer begins with a complex series of steps. alternately stepping forward with the head raised, and then retreating a few steps while lowering the head, a movement that is intended to create the impression that the lion is keeping a watchful eye for anything evil.
    V. When performing a traditional Chinese New Year's lion dance, several performers must fit themselves inside a large lion costume and work together to enact different parts of the dance.

    The BEST order is:

    A. V, III, IV, II, I   B. III, IV, II, V, I   C. III, I, V, IV, II   D. IV, II, III, V, I

13.
   I. For many years the shell of the chambered nautilus was treasured in Europe for its beauty and intricacy, but collectors were unaware that they were in possession of the structure that marked a "missing link" in the evolution of marine mollusks.
   II. The nautilus, however, evolved a series of enclosed chambers in its shell, and invented a new use for the structure: the shell began to serve as a buoyancy device.
   III. Equipped with this new flotation device, the nautilus did not need the single, muscular foot of its predecessors, but instead developed flaps, tentacles, and a gentle form of jet propulsion that transformed it into the first mollusk able to take command of its own density and explore a three-dimensional world.
   IV. By pumping and adjusting air pressure into the chambers, the nautilus could spend the day resting on the bottom, and then rise toward the surface at night in search of food.
   V. The nautilus shell looks like a large snail shell, similar to those of its ancestors, who used their shells as protective coverings while they were anchored to the sea floor.
   The BEST order is:
   A. V, II, IV, I, III   B. V, I, II, III, IV   C. I, II, V, III, IV   D. I, V, II, IV, III

14.
   I. While France and England battled for control of the region, the Acadiens prospered on the fertile farmland, which was finally secured by England in 1713.
   II. Early in the 17th century, settlers from Western France founded a colony called Acadie in what is now the Canadian province of Nova Scotia.
   III. At this time, English officials feared the presence of spies among the Acadiens who might be loyal to their French homeland, and the Acadiens were deported to spots along the Atlantic and Caribbean shores of America.
   IV. The French settlers remained on this land, under English rule, for around forty years, until the beginning of the French and Indian War, another conflict between France and England.
   V. As the Acadien refugees drifted toward a final home in Southern Louisiana, neighbors shortened their name to "Cadien," and finally "Cajun," the name which the descendants of early Acadiens still call themselves.
   The BEST order is:
   A. I, IV, II, III, V   B. II, I, III, V, IV   C. II, I, IV, III, V   D. V, II, III, IV, I

15.
   I. Traditional households in the Eastern and Western regions of Africa serve two meals a day—one at around noon, and the other in the evening.
   II. The starch is then used in the way that Americans might use a spoon, to scoop up a portion of the main dish on the person's plate.
   III. The reason for the starch's inclusion in every meal has to do with taste as well as nutrition; African food can be very spicy, and the starch is known to cool the burning effect of the main dish.
   IV. When serving these meals, the main dish is usually served on individual plates, and the starch is served on a communal plate, from which diners break off a piece of bread or scoop rice or fufu in their fingers.

V. The typical meals usually consist of a thick stew or soup as the main course, and an accompanying starch—either bread, rice, or *fufu*, a starchy grain paste similar in consistency to mashed potatoes.
The BEST order is:
A. V, II, III, IV, I B. V, I, IV, III, II C. I, IV, V, III, II D. I, V, IV, II, III

16.
I. In the early days of the American Midwest, Indiana settlers sometimes came together to hold an event called an apple peeling, where neighboring settlers gathered at the homestead of a host family to help prepare the hosts' apple crop for cooking, canning, and making apple butter.
II. At the beginning of the event, each peeler sat down in front of a ten- or twenty-gallon stone jar and was given a crock of apples and a paring knife.
III. Once a peeler had finished with a crock, another was placed next to him; if the peeler was an unmarried man, he kept a strict count of the number of apples he had peeled, because the winner was allowed to kiss the girl of his choice.
IV. The peeling usually ended by 9:30 in the evening, when the neighbors gathered in the host family's parlor for a dance social.
V. The apples were peeled, cored, and quartered, and then placed into the jar.
The BEST order is:
A. I, V, III, IV, II B. II, V, III, IV, I C. I, II, V, III, IV D. II, I, V, IV, III

16.____

17.
I. If your pet turtle is a land turtle and is native to temperate climates, it will stop eating some time in October, which should be your cue to prepare the turtle for hibernation.
II. The box should then be covered with a wire screen, which will protect the turtle from any rodents or predators that might want to take advantage of a motionless and helpless animal.
III. When your turtle hasn't eaten for a while and appears ready to hibernate, it should be moved to its winter quarters, most likely a cellar or garage, where the temperature should range between 40° and 45°F.
IV. Instead of feeding the turtle, you should bathe it every day in warm water, to encourage the turtle to empty its intestines in preparation for its long winter sleep.
V. Here the turtle should be placed in a well-ventilated box whose bottom is covered with a moisture-absorbing layer of clay beads, and then filled three-fourths full with almost dry peat moss or wood chips, into which the turtle will burrow and sleep for several months.
The BEST order is:
A. I, IV, III, V, II B. III, IV, II, V, I C. III, II, IV, I, V D. IV, V, II, III, I

17.____

18.
I. Once he has reached the nest, the hunter uses two sturdy bamboo poles like huge chopsticks to pull the next away from the mountainside, into a large basket that will be lowered to people waiting below.
II. The world's largest honeybees colonize the Nealese mountainsides, building honeycombs as large as a person on sheer rock faces that are often hundreds of feet high.

18.____

III. In the remote mountain country of Nepal, a small band of "honey hunters" carry out a tradition so ancient that 10,000 year-old drawings of the practice have been found in the caves of Nepal.
IV. To harvest the honey and beeswax from these combs, a honey hunter climbs above the nests, lowers a long bamboo-fiber ladder over the cliff, and then climbs down.
V. Throughout this dangerous practice, the hunter is stung repeatedly, and only the veterans, with skin that has been toughened over the years, are able to return from a hunt without the painful swelling caused by stings.

The BEST order is:
A. II, IV, III, V, I B. II, IV, I, V, III C. V, III, II, IV, I D. III, II, IV, I, V

19. I. After the Romans left Britain, there were relentless attacks on the islands from the barbarian tribes of northern Germany—the Angles, Saxons, and Jutes.
II. As the empire weakened, Roman soldiers withdrew from Britain, leaving behind a country that continued to practice the Christian religion that had been introduced by the Romans.
III. Early Latin writings tell of a Christian warrior named Arturius (Arthur, in English) who led the British citizens to defeat these barbarian invades, and brought an extended period of peace to the lands of Britain.
IV. Long ago, the British Isles were part of the far-flung Roman Empire that extended across most of Europe and into Africa and Asia.
V. The romantic legend of King Arthur and his knights of the Round Table, one of the most popular and widespread stories of all time, appears to have some foundation in history.

The BEST order is:
A. V, IV, III, II, I B. V, IV, II, I, III C. IV, V, II, III, I D. IV, III, II, I, V

19.____

20. I. The cylinder was allowed to cool until it could stand on its own, and then it was cut from the tube and split down the side with a single straight cut.
II. Nineteenth-century glassmakers, who had not yet discovered the glazier's modern techniques for making panes of glass, had to create a method for converting their blown gas into flat sheets.
III. The bubble was then pierced at the end to make a hole that opened up while the glassmaker gently spun it, creating a cylinder of glass.
IV. Turned on its side and laid on a conveyor belt, the cylinder was strengthened, or tempered, by being heated again and cooled very slowly, eventually flattening out into a single rectangular of glass.
V. To do this, the glassmaker dipped the end of a long tube into melted glass and blew into the other end of the tube, creating an expanding bubble of glass.

The BEST order is:
A. II, V, III, IV, I B. II, IV, V, III, I C. III, V, II, IV, I D. III, I, IV, V, II

20.____

21.
  I. The splints are almost always hidden, but horses are occasionally born whose splinted toes project from the leg on either side, just above the hoof.
  II. The second and fourth toes remained, but shrank to thin splints of bone that fused invisibly to the horse's leg bone.
  III. Horses are unique among mammals, having evolved feet that each end in what is essentially a single toe, capped by a large, sturdy hoof.
  IV. Julius Caesar, an emperor of ancient Rome, was said to have owned one of these three-toed horses, and considered it so special that he would not permit anyone else to ride it.
  V. Though the horse's earlier ancestors possessed the traditional mammalian set of five toes on each foot, the horse has retained only its third toe; its first and fifth toes disappeared completely as the horse evolved.

  The BEST order is:
  A. III, V, II, I, IV   B. V, III, II, IV, I   C. III, II, V, I, IV   D. V, II, III, I, IV

22.
  I. The new building materials—some of which are twenty feet long, and weigh nearly six tons—were transported to Pohnpei on rafts, and were brought into their present position by using hibiscus fiber ropes and leverage to move the stone columns upward along the inclined trunks of coconut palm trees.
  II. The ancestors built great fires to heat the stone, and then poured cool seawater on the columns, which caused the stone to contract and split along natural fracture lines.
  III. The now-abandoned enclave of Nan Madol, a group of 92 man-made islands off the shore of the Micronesian island of Pohnpei, is estimated to have been built around the year 500 A.D.
  IV. The islanders say their ancestors quarried stone columns from a nearby island, where large basalt columns were formed by the cooling of molten lava.
  V. The structures of Nan Madol are remarkable for the sheer size of some of the stone "longs" or columns that were used to create the walls of the offshore community, and today anthropologists can only rely on the information of existing local people for clues about how Nan Madol was built.

  The BEST order is:
  A. V, IV, III, II, I   B. V, III, I, IV, II   C. III, V, IV, II, I   D. III, I, IV, II, V

23.
  I. One of the most easily manipulated substances on earth, glass can be made into ceramic tiles that are composed of over 90% air.
  II. NASA's space shuttles are the first spacecraft ever designed to leave and re-enter the earth's atmosphere while remaining intact.
  III. These ceramic tiles are such effective insulators that when a tile emerges from the oven in which it was fired, it can be held safely in a person's hand by the edges while its interior still glows at a temperature well over 2000°F.
  IV. Eventually, the engineers were led to a material that is as old as our most ancient civilization.
  V. Because the temperature during atmospheric re-entry is so incredibly hot, it took NASA's engineers some time to find a substance capable of protecting the shuttles.

The BEST order is:
A. V, II, I, II, IV   B. II, V, IV, I, III   C. II, III, I, IV, V   D. V, IV, III, I, II

24. I. The secret to teaching any parakeet to talk is patience, and the understanding that when a bird talks," it is simply imitating what it hears, rather than putting ideas into words.
   II. You should stay just out of sight of the bird and repeat the phrase you want it to learn, for at least fifteen minutes every morning and evening.
   III. It is important to leave the bird without any words of encouragement or farewell; otherwise it might combine stray remarks or phrases, such as "Good night," with the phrase you are trying to teach it.
   IV. For this reason, to train your bird to imitate your words you should keep it free of any distractions, especially other noises, while you are giving it "lesson."
   V. After your repetition, you should quietly leave the bird alone for a while, to think over what it has just heard.
   The BEST order is:
   A. I, IV, II, V, III   B. I, II, IV, III, V   C. III, II, I, V, IV   D. III, I, V, IV, II

24._____

25. I. As a school approaches, fishermen from neighboring communities join their fishing boats together as a fleet, and string their gill nets together to make a huge fence that is held up by cork floats.
   II. At a signal from the party leaders, or *nakura*, the family members pound the sides of the boats or beat the water with long poles, creating a sudden and deafening noise.
   III. The fishermen work together to drag the trap into a half-circle that may reach 300 yards in diameter, and then the families move their boats to form the other half of the circle around the school of fish.
   IV. The school of fish flee from the commotion into the awaiting trap, where a final wall of net is thrown over the open end of the half-circle, securing the day's haul.
   V. Indonesian people from the area around the Sulu islands live on the sea, in floating villages made of lashed-together or stilted homes, and make much of their living by fishing their home waters for migrating schools of snapper, scad, and other fish.
   The BEST order is:
   A. I, V, III, IV, II   B. I, II, IV, III, V   C. V, I, II, III, IV   D. V, I, III, II, IV

25._____

KEY (CORRECT ANSWERS)

1. D
2. D
3. B
4. A
5. C

6. C
7. D
8. D
9. A
10. B

11. C
12. A
13. D
14. C
15. D

16. C
17. A
18. D
19. B
20. A

21. A
22. C
23. B
24. A
25. D

PREPARING WRITTEN MATERIAL
EXAMINATION SECTION
TEST 1

DIRECTIONS: Each short paragraph below is followed by four restatements or summaries of the information contained within it. Select the one that most completely and accurately states the information or opinion given in the paragraph. *PRINT THE LETTER OF THE CORRECT ANSWER IN THE SPACE AT THE RIGHT.*

1. Australia's koalas live solely on a diet of the leaves of the eucalyptus tree, a low-protein food that requires a koala to eat about three or four pounds of leaves a day. For most mammals, these strong-smelling leaves, saturated with toxins such as phenols and the oily compound known as cineole, are among the least digestible foods on the planet. However, the koala is equipped with a digestive system that is able to handle these toxins, trapping the tiniest leaf particles for as much as eight days while the sugars, proteins, and fats are extracted.
   A. Because eucalyptus leaves contain a large amount of toxins and oils, it takes a long time for koalas to digest them.
   B. Koalas have to eat three or four pounds of eucalyptus leaves a day, because the leaves are so poor in nutrients.
   C. Koalas have a unique digestive system that allows them to exist solely on a diet of eucalyptus leaves, which are generally toxic and inedible.
   D. The digestive system of the koala illustrates the unique evolutionary palette of the Australian continent.

   1.____

2. Norway's special geopolitical position—it was the only NATO country to share a border with Russia—drove it to adopt much more cautious policies than other European countries during the Cold War. Its decision to join NATO led to strong protests from Russia, and in order to avoid provocation, Norway's foreign policy had to balance the need for ensuring defense capability with the need to keep tensions at the lowest possible level. Norway's low-tension "base policy" made clear the nation's refusal to allow foreign military forces on Norwegian territory as long as the country is not attacked or threatened with an attack.
   A. Norway's "base policy," in spite of its shared border with Russia, is the work of a pacifist nation that should serve as a model for foreign diplomacy everywhere.
   B. When Norway joined NATO, Russia feared a ground invasion over their shared border.
   C. The "base policy" of Norway is a perfect illustration on how much of Europe during the Cold War was a powder keg ready to explode at the slightest provocation.
   D. As the only member of the NATO alliance to border on Russia, Norway was forced to adopt a more conciliatory foreign policy than other members of the alliance.

   2.____

115

3. During the women's suffrage movement of the early twentieth century, it was typical of many psychologists and anti-suffragists to automatically associate feminism with mental illness. In 1918, H.W. Frink wrote of feminists: "A certain proportion of at least the most militant suffragists are neurotics who in some instances are compensating for masculine trends, in others, are more or less successfully sublimating sadistic and homosexual ones." In the United States, anti-suffragists, finding comfort in psychology, concluded that suffragists all bordered hysteria and, thus, their arguments could not be taken seriously, 3.____
    A. The relationship between suffragism and feminism led many scientists to conclude that suffragists were afflicted with some kinds of mental illness.
    B. During the women's suffrage movement, anti-suffragists such as H.W. Frink tended to label women who fought for voting rights as mentally ill in order to dismiss their arguments.
    C. Responses to the women's suffrage movement are indicative of the tendency to label those who challenge the status quo as "Crazy" than to comfort their arguments.
    D. Most of the women who fought for suffrage during the early twentieth century were feminists who were mentally ill.

4. All of the earth's early plant life lived in the ocean, and most of these plants were concentrated in the shallow coastal waters, where the sun's energy could be easily absorbed. Because of the constant advance and retreat of tides in these regions, the plants—mostly algae—were repeatedly exposed to the atmosphere, and were forced to adapt to life out of water. It took millions of years before plant species had evolved that could survive out of the sea altogether, with stems that drew water from the ground, and a waxy covering to keep them from drying in the sun. 4.____
    A. After spending millions of years underwater, the earth's plants finally evolved ways of surviving on land.
    B. Most algaes today, because of evolutionary advances, are able to survive for extended periods of time out of water.
    C. Despite the fact that plants began as purely underwater organisms, they have always needed the sun's energy to survive.
    D. Land plants evolved from sea plants after millions of years in response to the gradual warming of the earth's atmosphere.

5. Because of the unique convergence of mild temperature and abundant rain (17 feet a year), British Columbia's temperate coastal rainforest is the most biologically productive ecosystem on earth. It's also an increasingly rare and vulnerable ecosystem: in its Holocene heyday, it covered only 0.2 percent of the earth's land surface. Today, logging and other development have consumed more than half this original range. 5.____
    A. The uniquely productive ecosystem of British Columbia's coastal rainforest has always been small, and has been reduced by human activity.
    B. Despite the fact that it is the most biologically productive ecosystem on earth, the coastal rainforest of British Columbia has been largely ignored by environmental activists.

C. The coastal rainforests of British Columbia have been nearly devastated by logging and other development.
D. British Columbia's coastal rainforest originated during the Holocene Era, but has declined steadily ever since.

6. The Roman Empire, which ruled much of the Western world for hundreds of years, was led by an aristocratic class famous for its tendency to drink large amounts of wine. Recently, an American medical researcher theorized that this taste for wine was eventually what caused the decline and fall of the empire—not the drinking of the wine itself, but a gradual poisoning from the lead that was used to line and seal Roman wine casks. The researcher, Dr. S.C. Gilfillan, argues that this lead poisoning specifically affected members of the Empire's ruling class, because they were the Romans most likely to consume wine and other products, like preserved fruits, that were stored in lead-lined jars. 6._____
    A. The Roman aristocracy's taste for wine and dried fruits, according to one researcher, is a cautionary tale about the consequences of overindulgence.
    B. While the Roman Empire's ruling class suffered from widespread lead poisoning, most commoners remained in good health throughout the empire.
    C. One of the most far-fetched theories about the fall of the Roman Empire concerns itself with the lead used to line the wine casks and fruit jars of the ruling class.
    D. An American medical researcher has theorized that the fall of the Roman Empire was caused by slow poisoning from the lead used to line and seal Roman wine casks and fruit jars.

7. In the second century B.C., King Hiero of Syracuse called upon the renowned scientist, Archimedes, to find a way to see if his crown was made of pure gold or a combination of metals. Archimedes came upon the solution some time later, as he was entering a tub full of hot water and noticed that the weight of his body displaced a certain amount of water. Realizing that this same principle could be used on the crown, he forgot himself with excitement, jumping out of the tub and running naked through the town, yelling "Eureka! Eureka!" 7._____
    A. Archimedes, in making his famous discovery, unknowingly contributed the word "Eureka!" to the English vocabulary.
    B. The relative purity of gold can be determined by the amount of water it displaces when submerged.
    C. Archimedes, after discovering the solution to a scientific problem while stepping into his tub, became so excited that he ran through the town naked.
    D. The word "Eureka" has become a part of the English language because of an interesting story involving the ancient scientist, Archimedes.

8. In the nineteenth century most Americans had never heard of, let alone tasted, an abalone, the marine mollusk considered to be a delicacy by many Asians, and undisturbed abalone populations thrived all along the west coast. When the California Gold Rush of the 1840s and 1850s brought thousands of Asian 8._____

immigrants to America, many of these people began to harvest the dense beds of abalone that inhabited the state's intertidal zone. The Asian harvests eventually brought in annual catches of over 4 million pounds of abalone, and as a result, some county governments passed ordinances making it illegal to dive for abalone in waters less than twenty feet deep.
  A. The Asians who immigrated to California during the Gold Rush harvested so much abalone from intertidal waters that some governments were compelled to limit abalone diving.
  B. Abalone diving was unheard of in California before the Gold Rush, when many Asians immigrated to the state and began to harvest abalone from the intertidal zone.
  C. The extreme shortage of abalone in California's intertidal waters can be traced to the Asians who immigrated during the Gold Rush.
  D. The abalone of California's coastal waters generally live in waters less than twenty feet deep, where they are not protected by most county governments.

9. Maria Tallchief, the daughter of a full-blood Osage Indian from Oklahoma, was America's first internationally celebrated prima ballerina, rising to stardom at a time when classical American ballet was still struggling to gain international acceptance and acclaim. Her innovative interpretations of such classics as "Swan Lake" and "The Nutcracker" helped convince critics worldwide that American ballet was a force to be reckoned with, and her glamorous beauty helped popularize ballet in America at a time when very few people took it seriously.
  A. As ballet grew more popular in America, Maria Tallchief became a phenomenon in Europe, helping to secure a worldwide reputation for excellence for American ballet.
  B. Nobody in America took ballet seriously until the beautiful Maria Tallchief became an international star.
  C. With her beauty and technical innovations, Maria Tallchief gained unprecedented critical and popular success for American ballet.
  D. Before the success of Maria Tallchief, there were not many ballet dancers in the United States worth noticing.

9.____

10. Early in the Constitutional Convention of 1787, the idea of a two-tiered legislature was agreed upon by the framers of the Constitution. The final form of each of the resulting houses, however, was an issue that was debated openly, and which was finally resolved by the "great compromise" of the Constitutional Convention. While the House of Representatives was intended to be a large, politically sensitive body, the Senate was designed to be a moderating influence that would check the powers of the House.
  A. The framers of the Constitution could not agree on whether the nation's legislature should be bicameral, or two-tiered, at first, but after the "great compromise," they devised a House and Senate.
  B. The Constitutional Convention of 1787 ended with the "great compromise" that gave the nation its two-tiered legislature.

10.____

C. After much behind-the-scenes dealmaking, the two-tiered legislature of the United States was devised by the framers of the Constitution.
D. The framers of the Constitution, after some debate, decided on a two-tiered legislature made up of a House of Representatives and a Senate that was less susceptible to regional politics.

11. Although scientists have succeeded in creating robots able to process huge amounts of information, they are still struggling to create one whose reasoning ability matches that of a human baby. The main challenge facing these scientists is the difficulty of understanding and imitating the complex process of human perception and reasoning, which involve the ability to register and analyze even the smallest changes in the external environment, and then to act on those changes. 11.____
    A. Even the most sophisticated robot is unable to imitate innate human abilities such as learning to walk, converse, or perceive depth.
    B. Because of their inability to process large amounts of information, robots have yet to achieve even the most fundamental level of reasoning.
    C. Despite considerable technological advances, scientists have as yet been unable to produce a robot that can respond intelligently to changes in its environment.
    D. Because robots cannot automatically filter out all extraneous information and focus on the most important details of a given situation, they are unable to reason as well as humans.

12. Thor Heyerdahl, a Norwegian anthropologist, had long held the opinion that the Polynesian inhabitants of South Pacific islands such as Samoa, Tonga, and Fiji had actually been migrants from South America. To prove that this was possible, in 1947 Heyerdahl made a crude raft out of balsa wood, which he named after an Incan sun god, *Kon-Tiki*, and sailed from the coast of Peru to the islands east of Tahiti. 12.____
    A. Thor Heyerdahl's 1947 voyage on the *Kon-Tiki* proved that Polynesians probably had common ancestors in South America.
    B. While Thor Heyerdahl's *Kon-Tiki* voyage suggested a South American origin for Polynesians, most experts today believe the great migrations were launched from somewhere near Indonesia.
    C. To support the idea that Polynesians could have sailed from South America to the Pacific Islands, Thor Heyerdahl sailed the *Kon-Tiki* from Peru to Tahiti in 1947.
    D. Thor Heyerdahl's famous raft, the *Kon-Tiki*, was named for an Incan sun god, and was so well-made that it made it from Peru to Tahiti.

13. During the Age of Exploration, after thousands of miles of open sea, ships entered the bays of the Azore Islands, west of Portugal, with tattered sails, battered hulls, crewmen weakened from scurvy, and cargo holds laden with the treasure they had gained on their long trading journeys. Spanish, English, and Dutch warships prowled the waters around the Azores to protect this treasure, sometimes even sinking their own ships to keep it from falling into enemy 13.____

hands. During these fierce battles, many ships filled with treasure were sent to the ocean floor, where they still remain, preserved by the cold saltwater and centuries of rest.
- A. Although they are now sparsely populated, the Azore Islands were once a resting place for every ship returning from a long journey to the Americas.
- B. Many treasure hunters and archaeologists believe the sea floor around the Azores, a group of islands west of Portugal, still harbors some of the richest sunken treasure in the world.
- C. Economic competition between the European powers was so intense during the Age of Exploration that captains would rather sink their own ships rather than let their treasure fall into enemy hands.
- D. The rich history of the Azore Islands has deposited a large amount of sunken treasure in their surrounding waters.

14. The Whigs, a short-lived American political party, were wary of a domineering president, and many of them believed that the legislative branch should govern the nation. In particular, Whig leader Henry Clay often attempted to bully and belittle President John Tyler into submission. Tyler's resistance to Clay's high-handed tactics strengthened the office of the presidency, and in particular gave greater credibility to all later vice presidents who happened to succeed to the office.   14.____
    - A. While U.S. politics was at first dominated by the legislature, President John Tyler shifted the center of power to the presidency, while laying the groundwork for the downfall of the Whig Party.
    - B. President John Tyler, a failure by almost any other measure, can at least be credited with contributing to the strength of the presidency.
    - C. Henry Clay, who believed in a strong legislature, failed to win much influence over presidents who were not from the Whig Party.
    - D. President John Tyler, in resisting Henry Clay's bullying tactics, strengthened the U.S. presidency and lent credibility to the authority of vice presidential successors to the presidency.

15. By far the richest city on earth, Tokyo, Japan is also one of the most over-crowded; most of its people are only able to afford living in extremely small houses and apartments. In addition to cramped housing, Tokyo's overpopulation has created a commuter problem so grim that a corps of "pushers" has been hired by the city, to stand outside crowded commuter trains and help pack people inside. Problems such as these are so severe in Tokyo that there has been serious talk in recent years of moving Japan's capital elsewhere.   15.____
    - A. Despite the example of Tokyo, there is no evidence to suggest that economic wealth and overpopulation are related variables.
    - B. Tokyo's prosperity has led to such overcrowding that the country of Japan has recently begun to consider moving its capital to another location.
    - C. Despite being the richest city on earth, Tokyo, Japan is seriously overcrowded.
    - D. The small houses and apartments in Tokyo, along with its overcrowded transit system, are a perfect example of how economic wealth does not always improve a society's quality of life.

7 (#1)

16. One of the greatest, and least publicized, legacies of Native American culture has been the worldwide cultivation of food staples through careful farming methods. Over centuries, tribes throughout North and South America domesticated the wild plants that have come to produce over half of the vegetables the world eats today. Corn, or maize, was first cultivated in the Mexican highlands almost seven thousand years ago, from a common wild grass called teosinte, and both potatoes and tomatoes were originally domesticated by the Peruvian Incas from native plants that still grow throughout Peru and Bolivia.

16.____

   A. Explorers of the Americas carried many native vegetables back to Europe, where they continued to adapt and flourish over the centuries.
   B. Today's common corn is a descendent of the wild Mexican teosinte plant, and potatoes and tomatoes were originally grown by the Incas.
   C. Without the agricultural knowledge and skill of early Native Americans, much of the world today would be in danger of famine.
   D. Foods that are today grown and eaten almost worldwide, such as corn, tomatoes, and potatoes, were first cultivated by the natives of North and South Americas.

17. America's transportation sector—95 percent of it driven by oil—consumes two-thirds of the petroleum used in the United States. With the 400 million cars now on the world's roads expected to grow to 1 billion by the year 2020, oil-foreign or not and other finite fossil-fuel resources will some day be conversation pieces for the nostalgic, rather than components of the nation's energy mix.

17.____

   A. In the future, most motor vehicles in the United States will be powered by an alternative energy source such as hydrogen or solar power.
   B. The continued growth of the oil-dependent transportation sector is outpacing the capacity of fossil-fuel energy resources.
   C. Our nation's dependence on foreign oil is a serious vulnerability that can only be corrected by increased domestic production.
   D. In the future, 1 billion cars across the world will be competing for oil and gasoline.

18. Althea Gibson, the first African-American to win the Wimbledon Tennis Championship, began her career by riding the subway out of her neighborhood in Harlem to 143rd Street, where she played paddle tennis against anyone who dared to challenge her. Since the Wimbledon tournament was played on grass, Gibson knew she would have to prepare herself by training on a surface that returned balls as quickly as a grass court. She found the solution to this problem in the gyms of Harlem, whose wood floors allowed her to perfect the rapid volley that helped her win two Wimbledon championships.

18.____

   A. Althea Gibson's tennis skills, including her famous volley, were developed in and around the inner-city neighborhood of Harlem.
   B. Althea Gibson had to leave her neighborhood to learn tennis, but to perfect her game, she had to return home to Harlem.
   C. Without the wood floors in the gyms of her Harlem neighborhood, Althea Gibson probably wouldn't have developed a volley that would help her win two Wimbledon tennis championships.

D. Although Althea Gibson achieved international fame as the first African-American to win the Wimbledon Tennis Championship, the path she followed to that championship was as unorthodox as the champion herself.

19. The greenhouse effect is a naturally occurring process that aids in heating the Earth's surface and atmosphere. It results from the fact that certain atmospheric gases, such as carbon dioxide, water vapor, and methane, are able to change the energy balance of the planet by being able to absorb longwave radiation from the Earth's surface. Without the greenhouse effect, life on this planet would probably not exist, as the average temperature of the Earth would be a chilly 5 degrees, rather than the present 59 degrees. 19.____
    A. The naturally-occurring greenhouse effect, by which atmospheric air is warmed, enables life to exist on earth.
    B. The greenhouse effect is a completely natural phenomenon that has nothing to do with human activity, and in fact it is beneficial to the planet's ecosystems.
    C. Human contributions to the increases in the greenhouse effect threaten life on Earth.
    D. In order for life to exist on Earth there must be some kind of greenhouse effect.

20. The religious and scientific communities have for centuries been at odds with each other, and held opposing viewpoints concerning the origin and nature of life. Progressive thinkers from both groups, however, claim that the two communities, in their ways of seeking answers to humanity's most important questions, share a common set of goals and procedures that would benefit greatly from a cooperative effort. 20.____
    A. Scientists and theologians will probably never agree on the origin and nature of life, though some progressive thinkers are trying to change the way the two communities talk about these issues.
    B. Though most scientists do not believe in God, progressive religious thinkers are continually trying to persuade them otherwise.
    C. Progressive religious and scientific thinkers have identified shared goals and questions that the two communities can work together to achieve and solve.
    D. Religious thinkers, who usually scorn such scientific theories as evolution, have begun to acknowledge the usefulness of science in answering important questions.

21. The administrations of Presidents Richard Nixon and Jimmy Carter oversaw an Export-Import Bank that was increasingly active in trade promotion, with expanding programs and lending authority. During this period, expenditures for program activities expanded to five times their 1969 rate, but the bank's net income dropped sharply—the low interest rates at which the bank financed its loan programs were lowering its profits. 21.____
    A. During the Nixon and Carter administrations, the budget of the Export-Import Bank grew to five times its 1969 expenditures.

B. Though the Export-Import Bank was very active during the Nixon and Carter administrations, its profits were reduced by its low interest rates.
C. Both the Nixon and Carter administrations demonstrated a lack of fiscal discipline that led to a declining net income at the Export-Import Bank.
D. Presidents Nixon and Carter both favored an activist Export-Import Bank, but while Nixon emphasized the function of trade promotion, Carter was more focused on making loans.

22. The Kombai and Korawai tribes of eastern Indonesia are known as the "tree people" for their custom of living in large tree houses, built as high as 150 feet above ground to avoid attacks from their enemies. These houses are built mostly from the fronds of the sago palm, a plant that also serves to produce one of the tree people's primary food sources—the larvae, or grub, of the scarab beetle. The tree people cultivate grubs by cutting a stretch of sago forest and then, after splitting and tying the palms together, leaving the palms to rot. 22.____
    A. The food-gathering methods of the Kombai and Korawai illustrate that deforestation is not a contemporary problem.
    B. The Kombai and Korawai people of eastern Indonesia relay on the sago palm for both food and housing.
    C. The Kombai and Korawai fears of enemy attacks have led them to build their trees high in the forest canopy
    D. Among the world's least-tamed native cultures are the Kombai and Korawai of Irian Jaya, the easternmost region of Indonesia.

23. It's no secret that corporate and federal information networks continue to deal with increasing bandwidth needs. The appetite for data—whether it's for internet access, file delivery, or the integration of digital voice applications—isn't likely to level off any time soon, and most information technology professionals allow that there is cause for concern. But emerging technologies for increasing raw bandwidth, accompanied by the streaming and maturing of transfer and switching protocols, are a good bet to accommodate the hunger for bandwidth, at least into the near future. 23.____
    A. There are two ways to decrease the demand for more bandwidth over computer networks: either increase the "raw" amount of bandwidth over an infrastructure, or devise more efficient transfer and switching protocols.
    B. Emerging technologies, aimed at the constantly increasing demand for bandwidth, are some day likely to result in virtually unlimited bandwidth for computer networks.
    C. Many different applications contribute to the demand for bandwidth over a computer network, and so the technologies that are devised to meet this demand must be many-faceted.
    D. While there is always a need for more bandwidth on large computer networks, newer technologies promise to increase the supply in the near term.

24. In the year 805, a Japanese Buddhist monk named Dengyo Daishi returned from his studies in China with some tea seeds, which he planted on a Japanese mountainside. In China, tea had long been the favorite drink of monks, because it helped them stay awake and attentive during their long periods of meditation, and Dengyo Daishi wanted to bring this practice to Japan. Over the centuries, tea-drinking would prove to be a custom that would influence nearly every aspect of Japanese culture, and Dengyo Daishi has long been considered a sort of saint among the Japanese.

24._____

A. Because of the cultural similarities between China and Japan, it was only a matter of time before the ritual of tea-drinking made its way from the mainland to the island empire.
B. Dengo Daishi, the first person to plant tea seeds in Japan, is revered among today's Japanese.
C. The Japanese tea-drinking custom was begun in 805 by a Buddhist monk who brought tea seeds from China.
D. Without the shared cultural traditions of Buddhism, it is unlikely that tea ever would have been imported from China to Japan.

25. Aztec women held a position in society that was far more respected than that of women in most Western civilizations of the time. For example, an Aztec wife was free to divorce a man who failed to provide for their children, or who was physically abusive, and once divorced, a woman was free to remarry whomever she chose. Perhaps the unusually high regard for Aztec women is best illustrated by the traditional Aztec religious belief that a special, elevated status in the afterlife was reserved for only two types of Aztec citizens-warriors who had died defending their tribe, and woman who had died during childbirth.

25._____

A. The rights and privileges of Aztec women demonstrate that they were more respected by their societies than women of many cultures of the time.
B. In the Aztec culture, women had the same rights and status as the most exalted men.
C. Though the rights of Aztec women were still generally inferior to those of men, most Aztec women were granted a high degree of independence due to their service to the community.
D. The relatively high position that Aztec women held in their society reveals the Aztec culture to be well ahead of its time.

KEY (CORRECT ANSWERS)

1.	C		11.	C
2.	D		12.	C
3.	B		13.	D
4.	A		14.	D
5.	A		15.	B
6.	D		16.	D
7.	C		17.	B
8.	A		18.	A
9.	C		19.	A
10.	D		20.	C

21. B
22. B
23. D
24. C
25. A

GLOSSARY OF MEDICAL TERMS (EYE, EAR, NOSE AND THROAT)

CONTENTS

	PAGE
ABDUCT ...... AUDIOMETER	1
AUDITORY CORTEX ...... COMPLAINT	2
COMPRESSION ...... EPITHELIUM	3
EQUILIBRIUM ...... FURUNCLE	4
GUSTATORY ...... INTRINSIC	5
LACERATION ...... MILLIMETER	6
MOLECULAR ...... OSTEOMYELITIS	7
OTOLARYNGOLOGIST ...... PSYCHIATRIC	8
PULMONARY ...... SPECULUM	9
SPHINCTER ...... TRAUMA	10
TRISMUS ...... VOCALIZATION	11

GLOSSARY OF MEDICAL TERMS (EYE, EAR, NOSE AND THROAT)

<u>A</u>

ABDUCT
  To draw away from the median line. When the vocal cords abduct, they separate.
ACCELERATION
  A quickening or speeding up.
ACOUSTIC
  As pertaining to sound or to the sense of hearing.
ACUTE
  Having a short and relatively severe course.
ADDUCT
  To move towards the median. When the vocal cords adduct, they come together.
ADENOIDITIS
  Inflammation of the adenoid tissue in the nasopharynx.
ALLERGEN
  The material responsible for an allergic reaction.
AMPLIFY
  The process of making larger or louder, as the increase of an auditory stimulus.
ANATOMY
  The science of the structure of the body and the relation of its parts.
ANGINA
  A severe pain.
ANGULAR
  Sharply bent; having corners or angles.
ANTIBIOTIC
  A chemical substance which has the capacity to inhibit the growth of or destroy bacteria and other microorganisms.
ANTIHISTAMINE
  Any of several drugs used to minimize an allergic reaction.
ANTISEPTIC
  A substance that will inhibit the growth and development of micro-organisms.
ASCENT
  A rising up. The amount of upward slope or elevation.
ASEPTIC
  Not septic. Free from infectious material.
ASPIRATION
  The removal of fluids or debris from a cavity by means of an aspirator.
ASTHMA
  A disease marked by recurrent attacks of difficult breathing.
ATMOSPHERIC PRESSURE
  The pressure due to the weight of the earth's atmosphere, equal at sea level to about 14.7 pounds per square inch.
AUDIOMETER
  Device for testing the power of hearing.

AUDITORY CORTEX
  The sensory area of hearing located in the temporal lobe of the brain.
AURICLE
  That portion of the external ear not contained within the head.
AUTOCLAVE
  An apparatus for effecting sterilization by steam under pressure.

B

BACTERIA
  A loosely used generic name for any microorganism of the order Eubacteriales.
BACTERIAL
  Pertaining to or caused by bacteria.
BAROTRAUMA
  Injury caused by pressure, such as injury to the middle ear or sinus cavity due to difference in pressure between the atmosphere and the inside of the cavity.
BENIGN
  Not malignant.
BIFID
  Clefts into two parts or branches.
BILATERAL
  Having two sides or pertaining to two layers.

C

CANNULATION
  The insertion of a cannula into a hollow organ or body cavity.
CAUTERIZE
  To burn with a hot instrument or with a caustic substance so as to destroy tissue or prevent the spread of infection.
CELLULITIS
  Infection or inflammation of the loose subcutaneous tissue.
CENTIMETER
  A unit of measurement in the metric system. Being equal to 0.3937 inch.
CEREBRAL SPINAL FLUID
  A clear fluid contained within the cavities of and surrounding the brain and spinal cord.
CERUMEN
  The wax-like secretion found within the external auditory canal.
CHONDROMA
  A benign tumor of cartilage.
CHRONIC
  Persisting over a long period of time.
COMMINUTION
  Broken into small fragments.
COMPLAINT
  The symptom or group of symptoms about which the patient consults the physician.

COMPRESSION
   The act of pressing together to diminish volume and increase density.
CONCOMITANT
   Accompanying or joined with another.
CONGENITAL
   Existing at or before birth.
CULTURE
   The propagation of microorganisms in a special media.
CURRETAGE
   To remove by scraping.
CYCLES PER SECOND
   In audiology, the number of sound waves passing a point per second.
CYST
   A sac which contains a liquid or semisolid material.

D

DECAY
   The process of stage of decline. The decomposition of dead organic matter.
DECONGESTANT
   A drug which reduces congestion or swelling.
DEMARKATION
   Any dividing line apparent on the surface of the body, such as the boundary between normal and infected tissue.
DERMATITIS
   Inflammation of the skin.
DESCENT
   A coming down, going down, or downward motion.
DIPLOPIA
   Double vision.
DISCRIMINATION
   The ability to make or to perceive distinctions.

E

EDEMA
   The presence of abnormally large amounts of fluid in the intercellular tissue spaces of the body.
ENDOLYMPH
   The fluid contained in the membranous labyrinth of the ear.
ENOPHTHALMUS
   Abnormal retraction of the eye into the orbit.
ENTITY
   An independently existing thing; a reality.
EPISTAXIS
   Nose bleed or hemorrhage from the nose.
EPITHELIUM
   The covering of the internal and external surfaces of the body.

EQUILIBRIUM
A state of balance. A condition in which opposing forces exactly counteract each other.

ERYTHEMA
A name applied to redness of the skin produced by congestion of the capillaries. This may result in a variety of causes such as infection and trauma.

EUSTACHIAN TUBE
A slender tube between the middle ear and the pharynx which serves to equalize air pressure on both sides of the ear drum. Named after Bartolommeo Eustachio, an Italian anatomist.

EVACUATE
To make empty; to remove the contents.

EXACERBATION
An increase or recurrence in the severity of any symptom or disease.

EXCISION
An act of removing by cutting away.

EXOSTOSIS
An abnormal bony protuberance.

EXTRINSIC
Coming from or originating outside the organ or limb where found.

EXUDATE
Material such as fluid, cells, or cellular debris which has been deposited in or on tissue surfaces. This usually is the result of inflammation.

F

FIBROUS
Composed of or containing fibers.

FILAMENTOUS
Long, thread-like structures.

FIXATION
The act of holding, suturing, or fastening in a fixed position. Direction of a gaze so that the image of the object looked at falls on the fovea centralis.

FORAMEN
A natural opening or passage, especially a passage into or through a bone.

FREQUENCY
The number of vibrations made by a particle or ray per unit of time.

FUNCTIONAL HEARING LOSS
Hearing loss without an organic basis, such as malingering or psychological.

FUNGUS
A class of vegetable organisms of a low order of development which includes molds, mushrooms, and toadstools.

FURUNCLE
A painful nodule formed in the skin by bacteria which enter into the hair follicles causing a localized infection.

G

GUSTATORY
Pertaining to the sense of taste.

H

HEMATOMA
A swelling containing blood.
HERTZ
The international unit of frequency, equal to one cycle per second.
HIVES
An allergic skin condition characterized by itching, burning, and stinging during the formation of a red papular rash.
HYPERACTIVE
Abnormally increased activity.
HYPEREMIA
Redness of a part due to engorgement of blood vessels.
HYPERTENSION
Abnormally high blood pressure.
HYPERTROPHIC
The enlargement or overgrowth of an organ due to an increase in size of its cells.
HYPERVENTILATION
Abnormally rapid and deep breathing.
HYPOACTIVE
Abnormally diminished activity.
HYSTERIA
A psychoneurosis characterized by lack of control of emotions.

I

IMPREGNATE
To saturate one material with another, such as to saturate gauze with an ointment.
INBIBITION
The absorption of a liquid.
INCISION
A cut or a wound produced by cutting.
INFECTION
Invasion of the body by pathogenic microorganisms and the reaction of the tissue to their presence and to the toxins generated by the microorganisms.
INFLAMMATION
The condition into which tissues enter as a reaction to injury or infection. It is characterized by pain, heat, redness, and swelling of the area.
INTRINSIC
Situated entirely within or pertaining exclusively to a part.

L

LACERATION
A wound made by tearing.

LARYNGITIS
Inflammation of the larynx.

LARYNGOPHARYNX
That portion of the pharynx lying between the upper edge of the epiglottis and the vocal cords.

LATENT
Concealed or not yet manifest.

LATERAL
The position of a part further from midline than another part of the same side.

LESION
A pathologic or traumatic lack of continuity of tissue or loss of function of a part.

LEUKEMIA
A fatal disease of the blood-forming organs characterized by a marked increase in the number of white blood cells.

LINEAR
Pertaining to or resembling a line. Linear acceleration means acceleration in a straight line.

M

MALAISE
A vague feeling of discomfort.

MALIGNANT
As applied to tumors, malignant means the tendency to invade surrounding structures and the ability to spread to other parts of the body by way of the bloodstream or lymphatic channels.

MALINGERING
The faking or exaggeration of symptoms of an illness or injury.

MALOCCLUSION
The lack of occlusion between the maxillary and mandibular teeth which interferes with mastication.

MANIFEST
Something which is readily evident or clear to the sight or mind.

MARSUPIALIZATION
An operation which removes a portion of a cyst, abscess, or tumor, empties its contents, and sutures its edges to the line of incision.

MASTICATION
The chewing of food.

MEMBRANE
A layer of tissue which covers the surface or divides a space or organ.

MENINGITIS
An inflammation or infection of the meningeal covering of the brain.

MICRON
A unit of measurement equal to 1/1000th of a millimeter.

MILLIMETER
A unit of measurement equaling 1/1000th of a meter or 0.03937 inch.

MOLECULAR
  Pertaining to molecules or a chemical combination of two or more atoms.
MORBIDITY
  The condition of being diseased or sick.
MORTALITY
  Death.
MUCOSA
  The mucous membrane covering a surface such as the membrane covering the surface of the palate or tongue.
MYRINGITIS
  Inflammation of the tympanic membrane.
MYRINGOTOMY
  An incision through the tympanic membrane.
MYRINGOPLASTY
  The surgical repair of a perforation in the tympanic membrane.

N

NECROSIS
  The death of a tissue or a part.
NEOPLASM
  Any new growth or tumor. It may be either a benign or malignant process.
NYSTAGMUS
  An involuntary rapid movement of the eyeball which may be horizontal, vertical, or rotary.

O

OBJECTIVE
  Pertaining to things which are perceptible to the senses.
OCCLUSION
  The relationship of the maxillary and mandibular teeth when in functional contact.
OINTMENT
  A semisolid preparation for external application to the body.
OLFACTION
  The sense of smell or the act of smelling.
OMINOUS
  Serving as an omen, or having a character of an evil omen.
OPEN REDUCTION
  Reduction of a fracture after exposing the fracture by an incision.
ORGANISM
  A body of living material. It may be a single cell, plant, or animal.
ORIFICE
  The entrance or outlet of any body cavity.
OSSEOUS
  Bone or bony.
OSTEOMYELITIS
  Inflammation or infection of bone.

OTOLARYNGOLOGIST
A physician who has specialized in the surgical and medical treatment of diseases of the ear, nose, and throat.

OTORRHEA
A discharge from the ear.

OTOTOXIC
Pertaining to something which is toxic to the ear. Specifically, certain drugs destroy the minute sensory cells of the inner ear.

P

PARENTERAL
Refers to medicine given by the subcutaneous, intramuscular, or intravenous route.

PARESIS
Slight or incomplete paralysis.

PATENT
Open, unobstructed.

PATHOGENIC
Refers to an organism or substance capable of causing disease.

PEDIATRIC
That branch of medicine which treats children.

PERCEPTION
The awareness of objects or other data through the medium of the senses.

PERFORATE
To pierce with holes.

PERIPHERY
Away from center. Example: The finger is peripheral to the elbow.

PETROUS
Resembling a rock. The petrous bone is so-called because of its hardness.

PHARYNGITIS
Inflammation of the pharynx.

PHARYNX
The tube between the posterior portion of the mouth and nose above, and the trachea and esophagus below.

PRACTITIONER
An authorized practitioner of medicine.

PHYSIOLOGY
The science or study of the function of living organisms.

PITCH
The quality of sound dependent upon the frequency of vibration.

PNEUMATIZATION
The formation of air-filled cells or cavities in tissues. Especially such formation in the temporal bone.

PROPAGATE
To reproduce, multiply, or spread.

PROPHYLACTIC
An agent that tends to ward off disease.

PSYCHIATRIC
That branch of medicine which deals with disorders of the human mind.

PULMONARY
  Pertaining to the lungs.
PURULENT
  Consists of or contains pus.

Q

QUALITATIVE
  Having to do with the quality of something.
QUANTITATIVE
  Having to do with the quantity of something, capable of being measured.

R

RAPPORT
  A close or sympathetic relationship.
RAREFACTION
  The condition of being or becoming less dense.
REVOLUTION
  A turning or spinning motion of a body or thing around a center axis.
RHINORRHEA
  The discharge of material from the nose.
RHINOSCOPY
  The examination of the nasal passages.
ROENTGENOGRAM
  The film produced by x-ray.

S

SALINE
  A solution of salt and water.
SALPINGITIS
  Inflammation of a tube. For example: eustachian salpingitis.
SAPROPHYTE
  An organism that lives on dead or decaying organic matter.
SEBACEOUS GLANDS
  Glands which secrete a greasy lubricating substance.
SEPTOPLASTY
  An operation to straighten the nasoseptum.
SEROUS
  Material which resembles blood serum.
SIMPLE FRACTURE
  A fracture of bone in which the bone does not protrude through the skin.
SPECULUM
  An appliance used to view a passage or cavity in the body. Examples include nasal and ear speculums.

SPHINCTER
  A ring-like band of muscle fibers that constrict a passage or close a natural orifice.
SPONDEE
  Two heavily accented syllables.
SPONTANEOUS
  Occurring without external influence. Such as the spontaneous recovery from an illness.
STAPEDECTOMY
  An operation which includes the removal of the stapes and its footplate, and placement of some form of prosthesis, such as wire, to take the place of the stapes.
STEROID
  A group of compounds that resemble cholesterol. For the most part, these drugs are used for their anti-inflammatory effect. Cortisone is the best known example of this group of medications.
STIMULUS
  Any agent, act, or influence that produces a reaction in the receptor.
STOMATITIS
  Inflammation of the oral mucosa.
STRIDOR
  The wheezing noise present on inspiration or expiration when partial obstruction of the larynx is present.
SUBCUTANEOUS
  Situated or occurring beneath the skin.
SUBEPITHELIAL
  Situated beneath the epithelium.
SUBJECTIVE
  Pertaining to or perceived only by the affected individual.
SUBMUCOUS RESECTION
  Excision of the cartilage of the nasoseptum.
SUPINE
  The position assumed when lying on the back.
SYMPTOM
  Any change in a patient's condition indicative of some bodily or mental state.
SYSTEMIC
  Pertaining to or affecting the body as a whole.

T

THERMAL
  Pertaining to, characterized by heat.
THRESHOLD
  That value at which a stimulus minimally produces a sensation.
TINNITUS
  A buzzing or ringing noise in the ears.
TRANSUDATE
  A fluid substance which has passed through a membrane or has been extruded from a tissue as a result of inflammation.
TRAUMA
  A wound or injury.

TRISMUS
   Difficulty in opening the mouth due to mascular spasms, pain, or disturbance of the 5th cranial nerve.

TUMOR
   Any swelling. It may indicate either inflammation, infection, or neoplasm.

TYMPANOPLASTY
   Surgical reconstruction of the hearing mechanism of the middle ear.

U

UNILATERAL
   Affecting one side only.

V

VENEREAL
   Due to or propagated by sexual intercourse.

VERTIGO
   A hallucination of movement. A sensation as if the external environment is revolving around the patient, or as if the patient were revolving in space.

VESICULATION
   Small circumscribed elevations of epithelium containing a serous liquid.

VIRUS
   One of a group of minute infectious agents which are too small to be seen under a microscope.

VOCALIZATION
   The act of making a sound through the mouth.